**The Law of Attraction: The S[ecret]
Magic, Money an[d ...]**

By Craig Beck

Copyright Viral Success Limited 2016

www.craigbeck.com

Download the free companion tools to this book at www.CraigBeck.com

Lao Tzu says

When the world knows beauty as beauty, ugliness arises
When it knows good as good, evil arises
Thus being and non-being produce each other
Difficult and easy bring about each other
Long and short reveal each other
High and low support each other
Music and voice harmonize each other
Front and back follow each other
Therefore the sages:
Manage the work of detached actions
Conduct the teaching of no words
They work with myriad things but do not control
They create but do not possess
They act but do not presume
They succeed but do not dwell on success
It is because they do not dwell on success
That it never goes away

Foreword

The Law of Attraction can easily be understood by becoming aware that 'like attracts like' or putting it another way 'you get back what you give out'. Sounds simple, but how do you make it an automatic part of your being?

An essential component of the Law of Attraction is realizing that where you fix your attention can have a powerful impact on what happens to you. However, despite what you may have been told your ability to manifest the life of your dreams has nothing to do with positive thinking and affirmations. Think anything you want but unless you believe it, you will not be sending the right vibrations out into the universe to have it appear.

You see, everything in the world is just energy vibrating at different frequencies. The sports car you want is just the same as you, a collection of atomic particles fluctuating at a precise frequency to generate it's physical form. If you want the sports car in your life you simply have to send out the intention resonating at the exact same frequency.

You may be wondering if this is all true then why do so many people continue to suffer with poverty, lack and want. Most people simply dismiss this theory as 'new age mumbo jumbo', but this is a law and just like any other it doesn't care whether you believe or not. The law of gravity applies its force on you regardless of what you believe and so does the law of attraction.

Even though there is a great deal of value to even merely finding out what the Law of Attraction is, this profound book takes you to an advanced level of understanding. In short, if you implement everything you read in this book your life will change more positively and dramatically than you may have ever believed possible.

You will come to be more attentive to underlying negativity and can begin to combat it with new beliefs and sensations that better reflect your constructive vision of the upcoming future. This ongoing focus on self-reflection also allows you to start seeing what you really want from your life, and you can then advance to developing clearer objectives with actionable steps at every stage.

Broken down into seven powerful chapters, each dealing with an important area of your life. This book has the power to deliver the life of your dreams but remember whether you believe that claim or not, you are right! If you can open your mind to a concept that has already changed the lives of thousands then you have truly found the genie's lamp!

- How to attract money using the law of attraction
- Living in abundance
- Find your soul mate and more love than you thought possible
- Manifest perfect health and vitality
- Ask believe receive

- Becoming fearless

Secret 1 – Manifesting Magic

"The Taoists realized that no single concept or value could be considered absolute or superior. If being useful is beneficial, then being useless is also beneficial. The ease with which such opposites may change places is depicted in a Taoist story about a farmer whose horse ran away.

His neighbor commiserated only to be told, "Who knows what's good or bad?" It was true. The next day the horse returned, bringing with it a drove of wild horses it had befriended in its wanderings. The neighbor came over again, this time to congratulate the farmer on his windfall. He was met with the same observation: "Who knows what is good or bad?" True this time too; the next day the farmer's son tried to mount one of the wild horses and fell off, breaking his leg. Back came the neighbor, this time with more commiserations, only to encounter for the third time the same response, "Who knows what is good or bad?" And once again the farmer's point was well taken, for the following day soldiers came by commandeering for the army and because of his injury, the son was not drafted.

According to the Taoists, yang and yin, light and shadow, useful and useless are all different aspects of the whole, and the minute we choose one side and block out the other, we upset nature's balance. If we are to be whole and follow the way of nature, we must pursue the difficult process of embracing the opposites." — Connie Zweig

Are you growing a little weary of watching other people fall on their feet and pick up what appears to be more than their fair share of life's riches? Perhaps you are so far away from what you think would be fair that you are currently struggling with debt and can't see a time when it will ever get any better.

Does it make you a bad person to want to escape the daily grind and struggle; is money really the route of all evil? The answer as you would expect from a book like this is a categorical no. The undeniable fact is money and wealth are just an idea, a creation of someone's imagination or perhaps a better label would be that of 'an illusion'. You see money as we believe it to be doesn't really exist. The dollar bills we see in our wallets are merely expensively printed IOU notes that promise we will pay our debt upon presentation of said bill. The debt never gets paid because money doesn't really exist. This becomes even more apparent when you deposit your cash into the bank and rather than store your personal currency in a special cupboard with your name on it (after all it's your money right?) your cash suddenly becomes physically invisible and changes to a series of numbers on a computer display.

You may be frowning at the book at this point and raising a fist to me while shouting 'it doesn't matter whether money is real or not Craig, I don't have as much as I want and that's why I bought your book'. Don't worry there is a good reason I am painstakingly going to lengths to make a factual if apparently pointless observation. Ideas are obviously just creations of the human mind and if we can agree early on in this book that money, wealth and therefore abundance are purely a creation of the mind then our journey to understanding why some people are drowning in the stuff and others are conversely up to their neck in debt becomes a whole lot simpler.

Let's be clear about something quite important, Manifesting Magic is not a course on how to become wealthy. The series of books you are about to read would be all missing the point of life if that were there only intention. Money gives you freedom – the freedom to do more, help more and give more. But if you believe that money will bring you happiness in and of itself then I am afraid you are in for a disappointing lesson in life. Money is not happiness, it is the merely the byproduct of achieving happiness. Over the course of these books we are going to discover how to manifest the life of your dreams, to find your true purpose in life and fill that hole inside you that has always been there.

If you currently don't have as much wealth as you really want or desire then I want you to see this as a simple sign that the hole inside you is still there. Desiring more money is a symptom of a bigger problem but just as you can't cure the common cold by wishing you didn't have it. You can't get more money trying to wish it into your life. Wishing is always an expression of scarcity and despite what your parents told you when inviting you to blow out the candles on your birthday cake, wishes are never granted when they come from a point of scarcity.

Money, wealth and attainment are not the point of this book but we start with money for two reasons. Firstly because the vast majority of people start this journey assuming that if they had more money they would be happier. Because that hole inside you feels like it needs to be filled with something, money and material 'stuff' seem like the perfect fit. The second reason for starting this series with money is to help people avoid the temptation to skip forward to find the 'manifesting wealth' section of the course. Let's be clear, there is absolutely nothing wrong with wanting more money and by taking this course you will be able to dramatically increase the amount you have and quicker than you ever expected to be possible. The really amazing news is that as exciting as that prospect may sound I want to tell you the other benefits are going to make all this extra wealth and abundance pale into insignificance. You are about to discover something profoundly beautiful and life changing. I am deeply excited to be here at the start of the journey with you.

Before we go any further, let's deal with some of the stigma attached to having and wanting money. Your elders, parents and religious teachers would have you believe that money is the work of the devil and only truly selfish and shallow people go off in search of it. Money is referred to as cold hard cash, which is 'nonsense'. Money isn't cold or hard, it's soft and warm and I don't believe for a minute that if I made my bed out of it I wouldn't have the best night's sleep of my life.

So why do some people have more trappings of success than other (often more deserving) people? To give you a really simple answer… we are all given two books of magic spells. One book creates pain, misery and lack. Meanwhile, the spells in the second book manifest love, wealth, abundance and happiness. Unfortunately neither book is labeled and the spells are written in a language that we don't understand.

The longer (and clearly necessary) answer is this. The world is a duality, everything is in perfect balance. Eastern religions explain it as 'yin and yang'. You can't choose to only have 'yin' in your life, you must also take the opposing 'yang' that comes with it. We often bemoan the unfairness of life and some people eventually use the struggle of life as proof that there cannot possibly be a loving God or divine creator. For if there were such a being he would surely not sit by and allow the suffering to continue. What we fail to see is that the things we want and desire in life could not exist without their counter position to give them context. As the saying goes *'even when you light a candle you cast a shadow'*. If everyone on planet earth had more money than they knew what to do with, would anyone give the slightest hoot as to how much something cost or whether their neighbor had a better car than them? Of course not, people want money because they have experienced (all too often) how it feels to have the opposite of abundance in this area. It is the very thing we hate that gives power and meaning to the thing we love.

Why do our loved ones die, sometimes painfully of horrendous diseases such as cancer and strokes? Again because without the concept of ill-health there is no context to being of good health. Try and think of one element of our existence that doesn't obey the laws of 'yin and yang', I know that you will fail this challenge. Everything is rotating in a circle, even the planet we stand on. There is no death without first there being life, there is no love with out having a polar opposite emotion to compare it to and there can be no happiness without the yang of sadness to give life to the state we desire.

Why do bad things happen to people? Because good things happen to people!

"If a man is crossing a river and an empty boat collides with his own skiff, even though he may be a bad-tempered man he will not become very angry. But if he sees a man in the boat, he will shout at him to steer clear. If the shout is not heard, he will shout again, and yet again, and begin cursing. And all because there is somebody in the boat. Yet if the boat were empty, he would not be shouting, and not angry. If you can empty your own boat crossing the river of the world, no one will oppose you, no one will seek to harm you…. Who can free himself from achievement, and from fame, descend and be lost amid the masses of men? He will flow like Tao, unseen, he will go about like Life itself with no name and no home. Simple is he, without distinction. To all

appearances he is a fool. His steps leave no trace. He has no power. He achieves nothing, has no reputation. Since he judges no one, no one judges him. Such is the perfect man: His boat is empty." — Osho

Within you there is a source of manifestation power that is capable of creating an abundance of anything you desire. This amazing and divine ray gun will amplify and magnify whatever you point it at. But here's the catch, there is no instruction manual and no safety switch. It doesn't warn you before you fire it and if you choose to point it at poverty that is exactly what you will get more of. So, you might think 'why don't people just make sure they point it at good things'? It's a good observation but it's not quite as simple as it appears. Noticing that your neighbor has a better car than you and deciding you want a better car as a result of this does not point the gun at manifesting an automobile. Instead the gun gets pointed at your jealousy and scarcity mindset. Rather than pulling up on your own drive a few days later in your new Mercedes you get more and more infuriated as you watch your neighbor get a pool installed and head off on his third vacation of the year.

The main reason we cast the wrong spells and point the magic ray gun at the opposite of what we want is we give control of the device to the voice that shouts the loudest. Do you remember being a small child at school when the teacher asked a question and you realized you actually knew the answer? Do you remember how high in the air you shoved your hand? So high that you had to use your other hand to support it and keep it defying gravity up there! Inside us there are two elements that direct the flow of our life. The soul (or subconscious if you would rather stay clear of any religious undertones) and the conscious or ego.

Humanity has a problem and quite a significant one; we perceive the ego to be a gift when in reality it is a curse. We believe the ego to be a unique facet of our individuality that gives us independence and character. The ego in reality is a fragment of our being that is quite frankly insane. Such is the insanity that it has even managed to convince us that bad is good and vice versa.

When we talk about the ego most people assume we are referring to one specific type of selfish behavior.
However, the ego is so much more that that narrow band of negative patterns and yet that doesn't mean there is a good side to it, no aspect of the ego can be viewed in any sort of positive light or considered an advantage to the human existence.
The ego really is the insane part of our physiological make up and absolutely nobody is free of it, not even the most enlightened being. We all have differing strengths of ego and ergo according levels of insanity that present themselves in a myriad of different ways that we might label as character traits or personality.

The first thing you should know of this part of you, is that the ego cannot ever be satisfied, it can only ever be sedated temporarily. Like a naughty child at the 'all you can eat' ice cream factory it will always want more no matter how much it gets, even if more of what you crave is in the long run detrimental to your well being. It is for this reason alone that giving a person the exact amount of money they have declared will bring peace is only effective as a temporary sticking plaster solution to their problems. Very soon reasons why that amount was too conservative begin to emerge.

Unhappiness, pain and misery are human emotions created directly by the ego to manipulate a desired response. These painful feelings are generated by the 'thinking mind' when it doesn't get what it wants but also rather ironically also directly as the result of giving it exactly what it wants too, such is the insanity!

Think of the soul/subconscious as silent but powerful and the ego as noisy but weak. Because the ego has his hand in the air and is screaming for our attention we get mixed up about which part of us is weak and which part is powerful. It is natural to assume the element of our being that is jumping up and down and assuring us that it knows what to do is the best holder of the ray gun. This is wrong, wrong, wrong – we inadvertently give the keys to the asylum to the most dangerous inmate.

The ego insists it knows how to use the ray gun to give you what you want. Like a baby who has just had its lolly pop taken from him, it will scream blue murder until you give it what it wants. But, your ego can achieve peace only for the tiniest fragment of time, normally immediately after you give it what it wants. For the briefest of moments it affords you a small break from the insanity and stops relentlessly punishing and manipulating you. When the sedation begins to fade the ego reawakens as ravenous as a grizzly bear stirring from a long hibernation. It demands more of what you gave it before but ten times stronger and will not accept anything but your capitulation, sending massive pain in the form of a hundred different negative emotions such as jealousy, low self esteem and self loathing until it gets what it desires. This is the exact reason why 95% of diets fail, trying to arm wrestle the egoic mind into submission with a technique incorrectly labeled as 'will power' is like trying to move a mountain with a spoon.

Nobody has ever achieved anything with 'will power' because it's an oxymoron there is actually no power involved in it at all! The ego cannot be strong-armed into submission by defiance; it has you outgunned on every level. Your ego has the power to cause you pain beyond your wildest nightmares and it isn't afraid to use it. The only way you achieve anything of significance in life and beat the discontentment of the ego is by harnessing the divine power of the subconscious. At this level of being you are capable of limitless joy, anything and everything is possible without the need for anything to make it possible. From mild contentment to perfect peace and everything in between your subconscious mind has the power to deliver it to you. This is what I call 'Manifesting Magic'; it is the other book of spells that you have rarely used. This book is in such pristine condition because you unwittingly asked the (insane) ego which book was best to use in order to get the life you want.

Until this point I have carefully used the word subconscious when really I would have preferred to say soul. I do this deliberately because for me to expect you to accept the word soul (and all its connotations) I have to make an assumption that you believe it exists in the first place. Virtually everyone accepts the concept of a conscious and a subconscious, I can comfortably bring these aspects of the human mind up nice and early in the book but I wait until this point hoping to have whet your appetite before I appear to go 'all spiritual' on you!

For me your soul and your subconscious are one and the same because what happens to you unconsciously and by that I mean without the interference of your ego or your thinking mind, happens with divine power. By divine I mean there is simply nothing that is impossible if your soul or subconscious so desires it. Naturally, the first skeptical objection to this grand claim of miracles is challenging statements like 'if I am all powerful, why aren't I rich already' and so on.

The deeper answer to that question you will discover as you journey through this book, but as a tempting morsel to keep you going; and of course to avoid 'question dodging' accusations flaring up so early in our relationship as author and reader I would ask you to consider that it is only your ego that believes you need money to be happy. Anything that has a its x solution in the future is pure speculation of your conscious mind, one of those specific requirements of how happiness should be packaged for your consumption. Your soul doesn't believe anything; it desires nothing, needs nothing and it automatically knows what will make you happy.

As a natural born cynic myself, I will try and answer your logical objections as we discover these secrets together. By this point I understand that your mind is probably acting like the Hydra beast of Greek mythology; for every question I answer two new ones appear to take its place. This is the ego again attempting to reassert its authority and we have been taught from an early age to listen to it.

From childhood we are told that to want too much is to be greedy, rich people are immoral and somehow tainted by their own success. Conversely to not have enough money, to be poor is also judged to be a failure. We project this confusing concept out to the masses through our movies, books, television news and tabloid newspapers. We love the underdog until they become successful and then we demand that they are brought down a peg or two.

Society wants us to have 'just enough' but not quite enough to be happy – this is what we have collectively agreed is 'normal' which for some reason when you write it down appears to be quite insanely ridiculous. Our parents also subscribed to this standpoint, as did their parents and all who went before them. It's the bizarre relay race of the ego forever passing its delusions onto the next generation. This is demonstrated by our parents in the vocalized desire for us to work hard and get a 'good job' to ensure our future happiness. What parents mean by a 'good job' is a safe and secure job that may even be boring but is continuous. Rarely do parents hope and dream that their children will follow their heart, throw caution to the wind and take risky, dangerous but exciting jobs.

There are many millions of people around the world in the most menial and insignificant of low paid, unskilled jobs that are content with their lot and truly happy within themselves, but no parent would wish or encourage this lifestyle for their child. Instead their aspirations for their young are generated from the ego and they dream that they will be the world's next doctors, scientists, accountants, managers and directors. Hopefully, along the way they will meet the man or woman of their dreams, settle down with a mortgage (a word derived from the Latin phrase meaning until death) have kids and live happily ever after, only to repeat the process again.

A list of handed down expectations that compound the belief that happiness is a destination achievable through the attainment or attachment to external things. They want this for us because it's what they want for themselves and therefore assume it is also the best that could happen to us. This belief is an oasis in the desert to the thirsty man, nothing but a pure illusion.

This cycle has been running in the western world for many thousands of years but recently levels of general unhappiness and frustration have begun to accelerate and magnify exponentially as a result of the stabilizing prop of traditional religion beginning to fail simultaneously. The discontented folk could previously be dissuaded from challenging the status quo with assurances that God has a place in heaven reserved for them, but only if they comply with the rules and dare not question the scriptures further.

In order to achieve abundance we have to consider the reverse of that position, as a result of this premise of human programming you will find that this book is not an instruction manual or a journey of discovery. If anything it's about the opposite of learning, an unlearning experience where we slowly strip away the false beliefs that you have been programmed and burdened with since birth.

When a fishing trawler gets trapped in a violent storm what brings the respite is the removal of something and not the addition of something. The removal of the storm and a return to zero is what dissipates the sensation of peril and danger. As such, happiness is peace and peace is the absence of everything else and so it's illogical to assume we can find what we are looking for by creating rules or by attaining material possessions. Abundance comes as the direct by product of happiness and is not the destination we are navigating to.

The secrets revealed in this course will change your life forever and your discovery of it at this point in your life is no coincidence. As the famous quotation goes; 'when the student is ready, the teacher will arrive' and for that reason, despite your excitement you cannot force this information onto others who do not seek it, do not expect them to receive the message with the same sense of wonder and excitement that you did.

Most people spend their entire lives trapped within the illusions of the egoic mind. However, a small and rapidly increasing number of people are awakening during their lifetime to realize the futility of their beliefs about what they think they 'need' to discover true wealth and abundance on earth. You are one of the enlightened few that are ready to discover that the universe always ignores the dreams of your ego. However, using the core principles described in this book you will soon be able to manifest your dreams quickly and easily using the power of your subconscious and your connection to the manifestation magic that resides within you.

Research shows us that of all the things you hear in a 24-hour period, 80 percent of them are negative. The average 18-year-old male has been told 146,000 times no or you can't do it. Now this causes us a problem because of something I call the law of subconscious attraction (or subattraction for short). Basically you have delivered to you what you subconsciously know to be true. If you simply know, and I do mean absolutely 'know' that you are an overweight individual then that reality will be created for you whether it's currently true or not. If at a subconscious level you fundamentally believe life is meant to be spent struggling to pay the bills and living hand to mouth (Perhaps just like your parents did) then guess what happens.

The egoic world in which we live would have you believe a whole heap of negative bullshit, because misery loves nothing better than company. In short eighty percent of the world is throwing a pity party and has extended you a big fat invitation. At the moment you are still on the guest list and what I am suggesting to you; is that if you change your beliefs not only can you leave the others to their depressing party but you can join the world's elite twenty percent who want for nothing and live the life of their dreams.

Now of course I am not suggesting that cash automatically brings happiness, but then the Manifesting Magic course is not really about wealth, it's actually about success. Wealth is purely the byproduct of that achievement and nothing more. To be successful and happy you must be a success on three levels. Spiritually, with your health and with your finances. If you are rich but your health is poor you are not a success. If you are spiritually connected and you are healthy, but you are poor, you are not a success. Get one area wrong and your life is completely different. These three essential elements must remain intact like the spokes of a bicycle wheel or the integrity of the whole structure collapses.

A frequently made mistake is looking at someone who is rich and assuming that they are therefore happy. The people who are the most content in life never set out to become wealthy, they just did what made them happy, what they were passionate about and the money just flowed in as an automatic outcome of their harmony with the universe. On the flip side there are many thousands of wealthy individuals who focused purely on the outcome rather than the journey. We all know that we could become fabulously wealthy in minutes if we would just pick up a sawn off shotgun and wander with some menace down to the nearest savings bank. For most of us we can already see that even if we did get away with the crime we still wouldn't be happy with our new situation.

So what is the foundation for financial abundance? Having enough money to live on and then some. More money than you really need. It's a very empowering feeling. Imagine thinking you can do absolutely anything you want. You really can be the best that you can be because you can buy any material, any service. You can go anywhere, any when x. That is what we are talking about with Manifesting Magic. The ability to be the very best that you can be. To have the very best that life can offer, the best healthcare, the best car and the best house. Everything designed to make sure you can live your life to the best.

Like everything solid you must build success on strong and lasting foundations. Life is about a chain of moments and your success depends on the choices you make in your daily actions. It's not about what you do as a one-off, it's not about that grand gesture that you just do one day. If you want to get fit you don't just go for a jog one day and then decide that you're fit, you do it every day. It's those actions in life that become habits that really change your life and move you forward.

I'm going to suggest to you many changes in this series of books. Even if you don't believe in them or you doubt whether they will work, I would like to ask a favor x of you. I would like to ask you to do them for just 21 days every day.

If after 21 days you decide they are not working for you, then that's fine. But I know they will work for you because after 21 days they pass from the thinking mind into the divine subconscious and become a habit. This new physical pathway allows you start to do them every day without having to make a conscious decision to do so. Before no time, they start to make a massive positive impact on your life. You'll see yourself turning towards wealth. You'll see your bank balance increase and you'll see your commitment to achieve that wealth grow day by day.

Happiness, peace and purpose are not things that are stumbled upon by the lucky few. All these states are the by-product of running a specific program in life. Yes, there is a recipe to success and if you follow it to the letter you can't help but achieve the desired outcome. There are FIVE ingredients to long-term growth and change and they are:

Desire; - and I'm guessing you probably have quite a lot of that. People who are not driven to succeed do not buy books like this one. I can't emphasize this enough; the fact that you are listening to this material speaks volumes about you and your intent. Truly eighty percent of the people you meet will never in their lifetime spare the time or the money to invest in a book like this. It's probably quite logical then that we know that twenty percent of the population own eighty percent of the wealth in the world.

Knowledge; before the captain of an ocean liner changes course he first must know in which direction the ship needs to go. Gaining the information you need is a fundamental step in the process of Manifesting Magic. Good news, investing in self-improvement audiobooks like this one is a clear indication how firmly on the path you are.

Skill; when you learn something new. Initially it resides in your conscious mind and requires active thought to complete the task. For example, when you learn to speak a new language, initially it's difficult and you have to think carefully about each and every word before you say it. Eventually over time you gain confidence and the process passes to the subconscious mind, at this point you have a skill and the once difficult challenge becomes an automatic process.

Action; doing what has to be done. That is so important because people put off things that are so important that they can't be put off. It can't wait until tomorrow. Your wealth must start now, this instance. If you stop the CD [transcription from the audiobook] and don't do something towards your wealth, you're wasting your time. You must take action and do it.

Applying these four simple principles to your life pushes you firmly into the top twenty percent of the western population. So many people go through life in a boring job they hate, nine-to-five, saying to themselves daily 'I don't like this job, I hate my boss and I can't wait for the weekend… but you know I play the lottery and maybe one day I'll win the big jackpot and then I can get started on living the life I want'.

Do you know how many of those people do go on to win the big jackpot? It's not many. For most forty nine ball lottery draws your chance of scooping the jackpot is over 14,000,000 to 1. In real terms you have much more chance of being eaten by a shark than you have of winning your fortune in this game of chance.

I have the good fortune to work in the media industry and I spend a lot of time coaching broadcasters and journalists helping them craft their on air style to appeal to as broad an audience as possible. Radio and television is a numbers game and these guys get paid on their ability to make real, everyday folk like them. The problem a lot of broadcasters face is one of lack of real world experience, they have always been in media, which lets be honest is a cushy little number. Most of them have never done a hard days work in their lives. They have never worked a real job and are faced with the daunting prospect of trying to be relatable to the very people who they have no experience of communicating with on a daily basis.

I sometimes tell them a story about my friend Mike, who works in a meat processing plant. Mike hates his job, beyond his friends who work there with him there is absolutely nothing he likes about his daily grind (for that is exactly what it is, a grind). People who love their jobs like the weekends but they don't see them as the only worthy part of a seven day week. Mike starts planning his weekend on a Tuesday, everyday in the break room he talks about what he plans to do on Friday and Saturday night. Then when the weekend comes around he finally feels alive, on a Sunday he tells me he stays up as late as he can because he knows as soon as he goes to sleep his weekend is over and another tedious week begins.

Don't underestimate how many people spend an entire lifetime trapped in this depressing routine, many never considering that there may be a way out of the loop. These are the eighty percent of the population who represent the bums on seats commercial radio and television stations see as their meat and drink.

It's this mass acceptance of a life full of scarcity that keeps generations trapped in poverty. Recent research has shown us that if you take 100 men aged 25, follow them through life and meet them again at age 65, do you know, out of those that have survived, how many are wealthy?

Five. Just five. That means up to 95 others are so poor that they're living on the state for the vast majority of their lives, and why is this the case? Simply because they accept the prescribed reality that life is a struggle but for a lucky few who one day might be lifted out of the despair by six multicolored balls dropping in the correct sequence.

These sorry individuals are responding to life as it happens to them rather than creating their own universe. This is like being given the winning lottery numbers but refusing to buy the ticket. You have the inbuilt divine power to manifest your own reality but you have to do something now. If you want to be wealthy take action, Today is the day.

The fifth ingredient to long-term growth and change is persistence. In other words, creating habits and not will power based goals. It's not what you do as a one-off, it's what you do every day that will grow wealth and abundance for you.

All five of these characteristics are necessary for long-term growth. If any one is lacking, long-term change will not occur at all. Many people try to take shortcuts around one or more of them, and the biggest problem is most people try to go straight from desire to action without pausing to acquire the necessary knowledge or skills.

In other words, people want more money and try and go and get it, but they don't really know how they're going to get it. Thankfully it's a little bit different for you because you've acknowledged that you need to do that and you've bought this audiobook. I'm guessing that this won't be the only MP3 or book that you buy on the subject. That's good. Keep going. The more knowledge you have, the more you have to use.

Some people do a little bit better. They'll go through the first three steps; desire, knowledge and skill but then they just can't get themselves to act. Or they accomplish the first four steps and then they get stumped when change doesn't happen all at once and they give up. They fail to be persistent. They fail to turn their new, good deeds, into habits. They're just one-offs. They get a little bit of progress and then nothing and they give up.

So remember, if the principles, questions and skills I offer you, are to result in long-term sustainable growth they must become habits. Nothing short of a habit will work for the long haul.

I am sure you have already read about 'The Law of Attraction', Rhonda Byrne's 'The Secret' and countless self-help gurus who advocate that the secret to manifesting the life of your dreams is hidden somewhere in their positive thinking mantra. Or perhaps after you have recited your positive affirmations enough times, only then you will finally get what you are looking for. I am willing to go out on a limb here and take a guess that you have tried all that 'stuff' and found it at best inconsistently successful. Maybe you got a little success but certainly nowhere near the life you dream of!

Of course, this is an easy prediction to make, because why would you be reading this book if the other stuff had worked the way you had hoped?

Why are some people poor and other people rich? Why are some people happy with a little bit of money and others miserable with millions of dollars? What makes one person popular and their company sought after and another despicable and avoided at all cost? What is the truth behind positive thinking and how can it help you?

The fact is that the conventional understanding of positive thinking and its techniques is misunderstood and misused by millions of people. It often produces the opposite of what you want in the first place.

I get annoyed sometimes when I hear people bleating on about positive thinking and how it can get you anything. You can get anything and you can do anything you want if you just think positively about it. It's absolute rubbish. I don't care how positively I think about it, I could not be a professional football player. I could not join the English Premier League and expect to keep up or perform on the same level as the other footballers. I don't care how positive and how many great things I say to myself, I know that I couldn't go up to an explosive device and defuse it and even dream of staying in one piece.

One of the best motivational speakers America ever produced, Zig Ziglar, summed this up perfectly when he said "positive thinking will not let you do anything but it will let you do everything better than negative thinking".

If you're currently doing a job that you cannot be positive about, you just cannot bring yourself to think anything positive about it, get out of that job now. You will never become wealthy or rich in that job.

Did you know that 80 per cent of the world's workforce hates their job? In fact hate probably isn't a strong enough word, they DESPISE their job. They turn up, they put their head down and for eight hours they hate, hate, hate their job.

Negative, negative, negative flows through every fibre in their body. That means that people on average everywhere are spending about 40 hours every week doing something they hate and trying to get wealthy doing it. It's stupid, it will not work. It's time to wake up and smell the coffee… You can only be successful in life if you're doing what you enjoy.

Why's that so? Well it's because you're performing the work of your heart and soul, what you enjoy. You create a special vibration with your thoughts and your emotions. Your thoughts become positive automatically, you don't have to work at it. You're always a positive thinker when you're doing something you enjoy.

If you are currently doing a job you don't enjoy, that you're doing merely to pay the bills and keep the wolves from the door, you will not become rich. It's not the way to success. Your job or life's work should not be something you hate, especially when it takes up most of your energy, your creativity and your life.

It's my deepest desire that with the help of this audiobook you will discover for the first time in your life what you really, honestly, truly want. That coupled with the practical application of the skills in this series of books to transform you into a shining beacon of happiness, peace and purpose.

Of course I don't know you personally, and the chances are good that we have never met. However, I believe that even without meeting you I already know two fundamental things about who you are, how you feel and what you really want to happen next. If you are anything like me, you will have always had a nagging sensation that you are here to do something important. You understand there is great potential inside you and life has an important mission for you. This sensation is what Nazi war camp survivor Victor Frankl described as the existential vacuum. It is literally a black hole in your being that is created by the failure to follow your heart and complete the task that you are really here to do. This hole is painful and uncomfortable, it is always there at the background of your existence and it won't go away until you fill it back up.

My brother in law once set up a business called SAHAFI. I asked him what the company does and he replied 'anything'. Being rather confused by his answer I asked what the name meant and he revealed that it was an acronym for 'See A Hole And Fill It'. This is an instinctive response of human beings and we approach this internal vacuum with the same sticking plaster approach. We know there is a dull ache inside us created by this emptiness and so we desperately try to fill it up. Our favorite ways to do this are with material possessions, sex, drugs and alcohol and all other things earthly and physical. This universally pursued attempt to fill the hole is as effective as trying to fill a volcano by throwing matchsticks into it. Fruitless, pointless and a waste of time!

How many people do you know who give everything they have to climb the corporate ladder, to get onto the next pay scale to get the car with upgraded leather interiors?

How many people do you know choose where they live or the car they drive by comparing it to what their friends and neighbors have?

How many people do you know who max out their credit card so they can have a television at least two inches bigger than their friends have?

Does it ever make any of them happy, I mean truly a genuine sensation of peace and contentment with life? Maybe for a few days, even possibly for a few weeks but never (and I really do mean never) for a lifetime. Money, cars, boats, houses, vacations, gadgets, technology and all this other 'stuff' we dream of owning are nothing more than matchsticks for the volcano. I don't know what your true purpose in life is but I do know that it is not to own a great automobile or only ever stay in five star hotels. Over this series of books you are going to discover what you need to fill that vacuum inside you. When the hole is filled you are going to find that love, peace, happiness and joy floods into your life. All the things that you thought would bring happiness, such as money, sex, vacations and abundance are not actually how you create happiness they are the result of being happy. The whole of the western world has got the whole puzzle the wrong way around. When you fill the vacuum then all the good stuff will automatically flow into your life.

I am deadly serious about this, there is no limit to the amount of money, abundance and love that can flow into your life just as soon as you start to travel in the direction you were always meant to follow. Let me ask you a question.

What do you want more than anything right now?

Whether that answer is physical or emotional, let me tell you that you can have it. But, only when you stop trying to force life to give it to you. Perhaps you want to meet the man or woman of your dreams. Maybe you have started to think that you will be on your own forever. Or are you one of those serial monogamists that go from one short and often dramatic relationship to the next, without ever finding that special person who you want to share the rest of your life with. Or perhaps you are the guy that never seems to get the break at work, missing out on promotions that you know you are more than capable of rising to?

Don't worry all these situations are just symptoms of the black hole inside you, pulling the exact opposite of what you want towards you. Once we fill this hole, the gravity of life will change. Literally, just like flipping a magnet the opposite way around, suddenly what was once pulled into your path will now be repelled. And all the good stuff such as the money, love, amazing relationships, success and peace will become drawn towards you.

You might be wondering why this book is spread over several short volumes and not published as one complete guide, as all my other books have been. Human nature causes us a little problem at times, we tend to be increasingly impatient and want the magic bullet cure for everything right now! We also tend to lean toward the incorrect assumption that happiness and success are a destination. That if we just 'earn enough money', 'live in the right neighborhood' or 'get the man or woman of our dreams' then we will arrive at nirvana. The universe is always expanding and nothing in life is fixed in one place. The tree that stops growing new leaves is a dead tree. So, to assume that if we struggle hard enough we can arrive at a place where all the bad stuff stops and all the good stuff becomes permanent is illogical nonsense.

One of my bestselling books is called 'Alcohol Lied to Me' and it has helped tens of thousands of people to escape the trap of alcohol addiction. The single biggest problem I have with this book is many people are so desperate to stop drinking that they flick through the book looking for the 'answer', the reason why the book gets five star ratings. Often they are disappointed because there doesn't appear to be a magic bullet. People get back in control of their drinking by using this book, not by reading one magical concluding sentence on the last page but rather by walking a journey with me through the entire book. Just as in life, knowledge is absorbed through the journey we take. I am pretty sure that what you have learnt since you left school massively outweighs the information your teachers tried to pour into your head by having you remember facts verbatim.

Life is about the journey and I am here to tell you that you will never arrive at the end. This series of books are designed to profoundly change your life, just the way the knowledge I share in them changed mine. It took me forty years of struggling to swim upstream in life before I discovered the secrets in these books. I was an overweight, alcohol addicted angry man who never quite lived up to his own potential. I suffered depression, anxiety and low self esteem for many many years. No matter how much money I earned, no matter how much I drank, no matter how many things I bought, the vacuum inside me just kept growing bigger and bigger.

Since I discovered the material you are about to discover I have lost over sixty pounds in weight, quit drinking, given up my boring office job (to follow my dreams of being a full time author) and moved to a beautiful island in the Mediterranean that boasts three hundred days of sunshine a year. I am forty-one years old and these days I step out of my villa pick up my surfboard and spend the days on the beach with the girl of my dreams. Yes, I am insufferably annoying to be friends with on Facebook… and so will you be!

Forget all that 'positive thinking' nonsense and the get rich quick notions of the 'law of attraction' and other such new age bandwagon chasers. Yes, you can really have everything in life you want but I will warn you here and now! The chances are better than good that what you are really here to do, what that vacuum inside you needs to be filled with is a million miles away from what you currently think you need.

Before you start on the second book in this life-changing course I want you to prepare yourself for what comes next. Just as a building without foundations will not be habitable you cannot turn your life around and start manifesting your dreams with the click of your fingers. Books and gurus who claim that the Law of Attraction and 'Reality Creation' is easy are not telling the truth. Sure, on paper it may appear to be easy, but the same is true when I watch my mother bake and decorate a beautiful wedding cake. As I watch the icing and decorative piping almost will itself onto the cake it seems like the easiest thing to do in the world. However, I know that the flow, expertise and precision of my mother's hand has come from decades of doing this artwork over and over again. I don't need to attempt to replicate her work to know that it would be an abomination of a creation. Yes, in theory manifesting magic is easy but this is only if you have changed your whole mindset and approach to life first – this part is not easy. What most people want is to get to the end of a book and then magically have a secret spell that will give them anything that they want the next day. If you are expecting this to happen I am afraid you have the wrong book, but worse than that – you will probably spend a lot of time and money trying to find something that does not exist.

There is an often-quoted saying 'thoughts become things', this is the cornerstone of books such as The Secret. The principle is simple; you get what you think about the most. So, if you think like a wealthy person you will become wealthy and so on. There is a slight problem with this theory and that is, it is completely wrong and doesn't work. Let me tell you why; thoughts are predominately generated by your ego (the insane part of you) but the ego doesn't have the power to manifest (or attract if you prefer). A thought in of itself is powerless, unless it becomes a belief. Essentially thoughts are conscious and beliefs are subconscious. For example you don't have to constantly remind yourself not to jump off tall buildings – you have a deeply embedded belief that this would be dangerous and most likely fatal behavior. Your subconscious protects you from the wild rambling desires of your ego by ignoring virtually everything it says. This is a very good thing – how many times have you caught yourself wishing harm to someone who has hurt you in some way (a cheating ex or a pressuring boss) only to calm down and realize violence wouldn't have helped. If your subconscious listened to every command of your ego the chances are you would be reading this from inside a prison cell, perhaps with me as your cellmate.

Before you begin the second book of this series I would like you to spend a week doing something very important. I want you to become aware of your ego. It's imperative that you recognize where your desires and motivations are coming from. The reason we do this is to reduce the power of this part of you, to make space for you to hear the silence of your subconscious. In that silence is the answer to all of your most key questions, we just never stop to listen to what is waiting to be said. In fact most people go their entire lifetime without ever hearing the message that could have changed their life. The voice of the ego is so constant that we come to believe that this is who we are. The voice in our head passing judgment and demanding this or that is NOT who we are, it is an illusion.

But how do I know when my ego is speaking?

This is really simple – any thought or statement that begins with 'I' is the voice of your ego!

- *I drive a Mercedes.*
- *I will only ever stay in 5 star hotels.*
- *I won't accept people disrespecting me.*
- *I don't think she is good enough for him.*
- *I expect good service when I dine out.*
- *I deserve the promotion more than him.*

We all think we know who we are, but really most of the things that we decide to label ourselves with are purely statements of the ego. Even positive marques such as 'I am a great parent', 'I am a dedicated employee' or 'I am a loyal and reliable friend' – all these pronouncements come from a part of our mind that is unstable. The ego lives only in the conscious mind and every time you make a statement that begins with the word 'I', you can be sure it was created by some false belief in this part of your physical being.

All statements of 'I' are subjective and as such are pointless. Our body and mind are not who we are but rather just things we own for a short while. When people ask me what I do for a living I answer by saying 'I am an author'. But is that really who I am, I think not. The ego cannot cope having questions left unanswered and so we are forced to find comfort in applying a label to describe our reason to be. Then we become attached to this security blanket and set about embedding in deeper into our identification with life. Photographers get up each morning and take photographs – because that's what the label dictates. This is how we can spend an entire lifetime avoiding the point of life. Eventually we become so attached to the label that our ego tries to own it. We start to compete with other people who have selected the same direction as us. We need proof that we are the best, first, quickest or any illusionary piece of evidence that suggest we have achieved permanency in our label.

A person might proudly declare 'I give generously to charity, I am a good person'. We know this is pronouncement is the pointless bleating of the ego. Money is relative, if a billionaire makes a million dollar donation and at the same time a homeless man gives ten bucks, all the money he has – who is the more generous. The correct answer is neither, because any judgment on that is still just an assessment of the ego, which as I have already told you is insane!

All pain and suffering is created directly by this part of us and by our instance on laying claim to labels. On a personal level it can be felt in the sensation of jealously we experience when our neighbor pulls onto his driveway with a brand new sports car. On a global level it has been demonstrated countless times when nations declare war on each other. Mostly these acts of violence erupt when one country attempts to take something that another country has declared that it owns.

The ego is tiny and yet believes itself to be big and powerful. The subconscious is infinite but believes nothing at all. It feels no need to question or judge, it simply does.

We are prevented from consciously accessing this limitless and divine power because we can't be trusted not to act like complete power crazy, narcissistic idiots. Apart from that we would be likely to kill ourselves in seconds as the ego assures us that it knows what it is doing as it lifts the hood on the engine that beats our heart and fills our lungs with air. This is the same voice that assures us that we don't need to read the instruction manual when we buy a new piece of electronic equipment or flat pack furniture. I don't trust this voice any more than I trusted my friend at school who insisted that washing powder has the same effect as cocaine. He spent the afternoon in the hospital foaming from the nose.

We can only access the power of the subconscious by two very different methods. Firstly, it can be achieved through a lifetime of deep meditation and constant cleaning of the mind. Most people don't have the patience or dedication to take this route. However, the second route is practiced by us all and everyday. Repetition is how we fool the gatekeeper of the subconscious into allowing us access to this amazing super computer. The conscious mind is so limited that it can only complete one task at a time and so when we do something often enough the mind creates a physical pathway to complete this function automatically, thus freeing up processing power for other tasks. This would be a fantastic benefit of the human mind if we only did things that were founded in love and respect for ourselves and other people. For example if you started a routine of ringing your mother at 9am each morning and telling her that you love her. After a while you would not even have to think about it, at 9am you would gravitate towards the phone and start dialing even if you were thinking about doing something completely different.

Sadly we don't always tend to use this power for good. We prefer to repeatedly stick cigarettes in our mouth, eat junk food and drink alcohol until we feel ill. These are the programs that we allow to inadvertently bleed though into our subconscious. Once past the gatekeeper and inside there are no further filters to protect us, as this part of the mind does not judge or question, it only completes.

Secret 2 - The Spokes of The Wheel

"The best and most beautiful things in the world cannot be seen or even touched - they must be felt with the heart", Helen Keller

Most people who discover these books have already heard of the law of attraction through other mainstream works such as "The Secret" and most of those people have had limited success so far. In Part 2 of Manifesting Magic I am going to show you exactly why that is and how you become one of the happy people who discover the real secret *behind* the secret. Wait, I am not saying my books are better that Rhonda Byrne's books, you will soon see that our judgments of good, bad, better, worse, richer, poorer and so on are all statements that are rendered redundant by the vastness of the subjectivity we can apply to their meaning. Something that I label 'good', you might describe as being 'bad'. Yet the thing that we are attempting to pigeonhole remains static. So, is the thing really 'good' or 'bad'? Of course the answer is: it is neither. This is an important point because it is this instance of human beings to 'label' things that prevents the magic of life from flowing. Essentially what I am saying is, because we 'think' we know best we actually make life the struggle that we desperately wish that it wasn't.

Imagine you are driving down the highway, happily singing along to the radio and merrily making your way to work. When suddenly out of the blue another driver cuts you off so badly that you have to swerve to avoid a collision. To make matters worse the driver in front doesn't even acknowledge you, never mind offering any sort of apology. If you are like most people you may shout and perhaps even swear at the offending driver. You may beep your horn and gesture with your hands and mouth what you think about this selfish, inconsiderate and dangerous moron, hoping that he is lip reading through his mirror. But wait, all is not what it seems. As you get closer you realize that the driver of the car in front is actually someone you know, someone you love. Perhaps it's your mother, your brother or your best friend. Suddenly with this realization your anger instantly disappears and you laugh. In a split second the driver of that car has changed from being 'a dangerous, selfish idiot' to a 'silly but lovable person, who didn't mean any harm'. The driving behavior remains the same but our opinion of it alters. We don't just reserve this inconsistency for our friends and family, we also tend to judge ourselves less harshly too. Let's switch the roles around, imagine if it was you driving dangerously and you who accidentally cut another driver off. You might witness the abuse being gestured towards you by the other driver and think 'jeez calm down, it was only an accident – wow that guy has real anger issues'.

What if we treated everyone like they were someone we loved? What would happen to your life if the next time someone cut you off on the highway you smiled and laughed at the silly driving of the car in front. Is it possible that life would feel less stressful?

Of course, it's hard to imagine us being so angry and aggressive with someone we love. But we must ask the question, if it is not the specific offense that upsets us but rather the person committing it why do we respond even before we know whom we are blaming? Also, why do we have this universal ability to instantly change our view of an event when we discover the person responsible for it is someone we know? How is it possible to take one piece of driving behavior and judge it to be dangerous and antisocial with one breath and then to label the same behavior as careless but inoffensive with the next breath? The answer is simple… ego. That little voice inside your head that judges and questions everything you see, hear, feel or do. As I told you in *Manifesting Magic Book One*, the ego is insane and yet we give it full control of our emotions and responses to life.

If you are an atheist or a devout follower of a traditional religion you may find some of the concepts in this book problematic, and for that I apologize in advance. I am writing this with a very open-minded and inquisitive reader in mind. I am making a few assumptions about you:

1. *You are open to the possibility that there is something very powerful inside us.*
2. *You believe there is something for us beyond our death, but perhaps you are not quite sure what that is.*

3. *You are open minded enough to consider that we existed before our birth and that perhaps our time on earth is an illusion.*

Many believe that our earthly body is merely a container for our true eternal self. Something for the soul to reside in while it explores the physical world. Our hearts are limited to a certain number of beats and our joints will make only so many movements before they fail. The ego is a part of the physical body but unlike your heart, lungs and joints this part of you has intelligence and is aware of its own existence. This knowledge is painful to your ego because it knows that it is a temporary physical entity, essentially nothing more than a piece of meat inside your head! It knows only too well that your body is a fleeting vessel, nothing more than a container for your soul. Your body will expire and ergo so will your ego. This prospect is terrifying to your ego and in a futile attempt to avoid the inevitable it will spend your entire lifetime kicking and screaming right up until the end (If you allow it to do so). Every negative feeling, thought and deed you have ever had was created by the ego desperately trying to prove the impossible. Your ego wants to live forever, why? Because it believes you and your earthly form are the most important 'thing' that has ever been created. That image you see looking back in the bathroom mirror is the reason for everything, the pinnacle achievement of the universe – there simply must never be a time when this concept does not exist.

The ego attempts to create permanency wherever it can, all in order to prove that it can cement your existence in place. It says to you that you deserve to own 'stuff', as much 'stuff' as possible. It will tell you that you should have an expensive automobile… How good should this car be? Well certainly better than your neighbor's car for a start. Your ego believes you should own your own house and we even have long established sayings to back up this dream such as 'a man's home is his castle' and 'always put your money in bricks and mortar'. Couples fall in love and the ego gets attached to this and insists you protect against it being taken away. These happy people get married and promise to love each other exclusively forever more – the ego adores the concept of marriage because it implies that love, sex, security and caring (all things it cares for very much) can be made permanent features of your life. Heck, you even have a legal contract to prove that it can't be taken away right?

Whenever I am home, in the little North Eastern town that I was born in and grew up in I always make a point of driving across town to Eldon Street. I drive through the town center and down North Road and towards the rows of terraced housing built to accommodate the community of steel workers who labored in the various factories and forges around the area. I turn left at the little store that was a video rental shop when I was a child and make my way to the very top of Eldon Street. I drive slowly past the bingo hall and its large tarmacadam car park, still the 'no ball games' signs are blissfully ignored by the children who live and play on the street.

When the numbers of the houses get to one hundred my heart starts to beat a little quicker and I slow the car to a snails pace. Eventually I come to a stop outside one hundred and thirty two Eldon Street. I pull on the parking break and sit in silence looking at the building. I glance at the small, red brick wall that my Grandmother would lean against as she made small talk with passing neighbors in the street. I notice the bay window, and while the curtains are different now, I still expect to see them twitch and move to the side as my Grandfather hears the approach of my car and looks out the check that it is me. I recall watching old black and white movies, westerns and comedies by Laurel & Hardy and Abbot and Costello while sitting on my Granddad's knee. Memories wash over me and fill me with joy and sadness in equal measure. Joy that these two beautiful people were in my life and took such an active role in shaping who I am as a person. Sadness that I was too young to appreciate that they wouldn't be in my life forever. You see, this is my grandparent's house and it always will be in my eyes.

My Granddad Jack Prest was a steel worker at the local rolling mills, a job he started at the age of 14. Initially making railway tracks, this switched to the manufacture of ammunition when the Second World War came about. He continued there six days a week until he was sixty-two years old. Sometime before I was born there was a great celebration in the Prest household as they achieved what many saw to be the pinnacle achievement for any workingman. They had struggled, scrimped and saved and now were able to move out of rented accommodation and were to buy their own house, *One Three Two* Eldon Street was to be their castle. No more paying rent to the landlord, this set of bricks and mortar belonged to Mr and Mrs J Prest, and they had the deeds to prove it.

In 1989 my Grandmother Lilly died and for the first time I saw this giant of an invincible man cry. I had never seen my Granddad cry before; it was a shock to see. I had seen him cut his hands open on sheet metal and not even flinch. If there was any emotion in those moments of pain it was more annoyance that the blood was making a mess. He was unbreakable, pure power and surely (in my opinion) destined to exist forever – nothing could take down my Grandad Jack. With the death of my grandmother, 132 Eldon Street became just Granddad's house and with the mortgage paid off he could now claim it was truly his house.

My Grandparents thought it was their house; then my granddad thought it was his house and now some other family have the paperwork to claim it is their home. All these people believed in the permanency of home ownership, so who really owns one hundred and thirty two Eldon Street, Darlington?

The answer to that question is the reason this book exists. We spend a lifetime striving to attain 'stuff', own things, climb the corporate and social ladders and to demonstrate our significance to others. But how many of us are happy as a result of doing this? I know from experience that during one of the wealthiest periods in my life I was the most unhappy I have ever been. I owned three houses, had an $80,000 car sitting on the driveway and only ever turned left when I got on a plane. Yet, despite all this 'success' I was miserable beyond description. Yes, it's true that the day that flash new automobile was delivered to my door I was grinning from ear to ear, having a little look around to make sure the neighbors were watching as it was lowered from the flat bed truck. But why didn't that happiness stick? I had been pretty certain that a new car would make me happy and it did, for all of a few weeks. But why did it fade, why did what I once believed to be the solution turn out to be just another red herring?

Everything we believe we need in order to be happy will only ever be like a shot of methadone to a heroin addict. A pale and temporary substitute for what we really want. Life is temporary, everything is temporary and to try and achieve happiness by attaining 'stuff' of trying to force the temporary to be permanent, by way of bricks and mortar or marriage contracts is as pointless as trying to bail out the Titanic with an egg cup.

The hard reality is that NOTHING in life is permanent, it really doesn't matter how tough the concrete and steel is that you build your home from. There will come a point in time when it crumbles to the ground and once again becomes dust. Saddam Hussein probably assumed his name would live on through the statues, highways and public buildings that he named after himself. But today despite all his best efforts Bagdad Airport is not called Saddam Hussein Airport. It's not just physical and material things that the ego tries to nail down and own. We are forced to experience hundreds of other negative emotions when we lose virtual concepts too. When someone insults us we lose face, when we ask a hot girl out for a date and she rejects us, we lose confidence or self-esteem. When our boss gives the promotion to the new guy rather than us we lose pride. The ego is terrified of losing anything because it highlights the temporariness of life. So, when that guy we don't know cuts us off on the highway we feel angry because it feels very much like he stole our piece of road. That bit of road is so obviously ours! In our mind it is our piece of road because we have decided to occupy that space and that is reason enough to get upset when someone else attempts to take it from us. However, it's hard to feel this anger towards someone we love and care about because we don't believe they are trying to steal from us, they simply made a mistake and we forgive them instantly.

My parents always told me that I needed to get a good job because 'life is hard'. This is a view the media agrees with and likes to portray on a daily basis, it is certainly still the view that my mum still holds. I am very lucky that in my entire life I have only ever been fired once, bearing in mind how terrible an employee I believe I am (far too free thinking to follow orders) this is truly remarkable. Nether the less, the day I was fired from hosting the breakfast show on Real Radio, in the North East of England was a real low point in my life. I felt hurt, rejected, unwanted and worried about how the event would change the life of my family and loved ones. Just like everyone else, when the chips are down and you really need some support I went straight to my mum for a shoulder to cry on. She hugged me close and again told me how tough and unfair life is.

In her unique North East accent she looked me in the eye and said 'Craig, life is one long bloody struggle… oh and your boss deserves all that is coming to him'.

It's not hard to understand why people believe this mantra so much that they pass it down to their children. Rolling TV news tells us on an hourly basis that life is harsh and deeply unfair. We sit and watch children starving in Africa and wonder if there is a God, how can he sit by and let this suffering continue. We hear about old ladies who have been mugged for the sake of their meager pension money and old servicemen who now sleep rough having fallen on hard times. Young lives are snuffed out way before they have chance to make a mark on the world. Sometimes by illness and often by drugs, alcohol or other tools we have invented to help us deal with this painful and cruel existence.

If you too have been told that life is hard and that you should expect to struggle through it, what I am about to tell you will flip all that on it's head – so much so that you may struggle to believe it. Life is only a struggle because we have given the steering wheel of life to the blind, mentally unstable lunatic with an inferiority complex. We have given all the power to the insane element of our being – the ego is delusional, terrified and demented, and everyday we look at this dribbling lunatic and say 'tell me what I need to be happy'! But what is even worse than that, we actually listen and try to get all the 'stuff' we are told we must have.

Here is the truth… life is not meant to be a struggle, it doesn't need to be hard and everything you need is already available! Yes, I know you are thinking 'this is just more personal development positive thinking bullshit' but let me tell you that none of this has anything to do with positive thinking, vision boards, mission statements or any other new age mumbo jumbo that has been dreamt up by some marketing team sitting in a plush Hollywood office. If you give the steering wheel of life to the captain instead of the deranged stowaway then there are calmer waters, plainer sailing and much less icebergs in your way. To get the life you want then you just have to let go of the wheel and let someone else drive for a while. Stop deciding that things are 'good' or 'bad', 'fair' or 'unfair' and trust that there is a part of you that knows what to do and doesn't need any advice or guidance from you.

What we have all been doing is jumping into the river of life and desperately trying to swim upstream. Our ego has assured us that if we can defy all the odds and arm-wrestle life into submission then we will arrive at a place called 'happiness'. As though it is some mystical town situated up river that only the strongest swimmers can get to. Your soul and the whole universe wants to go down the hill and if you stop kicking and go with it you will find it's not only easier but it's almost like every element in the world suddenly joined forces to help you.

The whole purpose of this book is to encourage you to stop kicking and trust that someone or rather something will be there to catch you. What I used to do (and probably what you are still doing) is so mind blowingly ineffective that once you see the truth you will be shocked you could have ever got it so wrong. In the past if I thought I wasn't earning enough I would start to worry about how I was doing financially. In the past I have moved us to a cheaper home, cut down on vacations and even traded in the family car for a cheaper or more economical model. This sort of reaction to life is what I call 'kicking', it is a negative ego created emotion that comes from the starting point of that there isn't enough to go around… BUT if we kick hard enough we might be able to get to a place where there is more. Kicking of any sort only ever moves you further away from where you really need to be going. Whether you are embarrassed about the shape of your body or worried about the state of your finances – these 'states' of mind are all kicking you further toward the things you don't want. Bob Proctor once said 'thoughts become things', and it is the sentiment behind law of attraction books such as The Secret. I don't think this statement is entirely true, it's not what you think that becomes real, but rather it is what you believe. If you believe that you are overweight and your body is disgusting then this will be the manifestation you inadvertently create. You will always remain in the state of being unhappy with your body because this is the program you have sent to be completed.

You have to stop kicking and I mean today, right now! But Craig how do I know if I am kicking?

There are two voices inside you, the only voice that matters is that of your soul and it gently whispers to you in just one language – 'love'. The second voice shouts and screams in a hundred different languages. Every time you choose to listen to this second voice you are 'kicking' up stream and moving further away from happiness, peace and purpose in life. The languages that this voice speaks are *regret, hate, anger, disappointment, jealousy, resentment, bitterness, selfishness* and any other emotion that doesn't come from the source material of love. If you don't get the promotion you think you deserve at work, feeling disappointment is 'kicking', resenting the guy who got it instead of you is 'kicking'. Now of course it's only natural to feel 'disappointment' if you don't get the job and you wouldn't be human if that wasn't the case. BUT the secret is to let it go, to stop kicking the moment you realize that you are. Sure you can say 'boy I can't believe they gave the promotion to David, he has far less experience than me! It's an absolute joke, gee I wonder what he has on the boss?' but this won't get you anything than more of the same. Better to say 'Ok, so I didn't get the gig. Maybe that's because something even better is just around the corner'.

It sounds simple right? Perhaps too simple to work?

Of course you might think that, your ego still has a voice. Your first challenge here is to let go of that thought and say 'but you know what, this is just crazy enough to work'. I spent the first thirty odd years of my life thrashing around trying to swim up that river. I tried it my way and all this fighting achieved was to turn me into a fat, alcoholic, broke, unhappy and angry man. The day I stopped kicking and let the river carry me to where it wants me to go I can't tell you how much peace and love just washed into my life. You have a choice here; you can take a leap of faith and trust me on this or you can walk away and declare this book to be just another self-help rotten tomato (no hard feelings). I have discovered the hard way how to get the life of your dreams and let me tell you that the universe is pretty happy with the way this system works and won't be changing it – regardless of what you think. This process is a law, just like the law of gravity. It is consistent and works whether you believe in it or not.

Can you imagine if you met somebody who didn't believe in the law of gravity? He was totally and utterly convinced that the moment he lets his tight grip on the earth slip he is going to fly off into space and die a horrible, lonely death. He struggles and struggles to hold onto something solid, but finally his muscles can't take anymore. The poor guy is exhausted and his hands finally give up the ghost and release his vice like grip… what happens next? Does he fly off into space or does he suddenly discover he had nothing to worry about at all, he is perfectly safe and suddenly he realizes that life is going to get a whole lot easier now that he doesn't have to struggle to hold on.

Towards the end of this book I will show you exactly how to stop kicking. Right now I want to take this concept a little deeper. If you have children you will notice that they use the word 'why' a lot. They want to know 'why is the sky blue?', 'why is water wet?' and 'why they can't have endless bowls of ice-cream?' They look at the world that we take for granted with new eyes and very little assumption or pre-judgment. There is genuine wonderment at the amazing planet they have arrived on. Slowly the novelty fades and we allow our view to be altered by the rules or opinions of other people. We are told that the world is a dangerous place, strangers are out to snatch us away, don't ask for too much because money is hard to get and of course to expect life to be a struggle. Before too long the child is no longer playing carefree and flowing down the river. They are stressed about their grades, bullies, teachers and the expectations of their parents – they start kicking in an attempt to get away from the things they don't want and in that moment the magic is broken. They join the rest of us, fighting our way through life.

You might be thinking 'but of course children will worry about their grades and quite right that they do'. You might wonder what would become of the world if everybody stopped kicking. I can tell you the answer – love would happen. If people stopped striving to own 'stuff', to be better than their neighbor, to have more then everyone would start to flow in the direction that the universe wants to us to, down the river and back to source. But why is doing nothing so powerful? We are repeatedly told that hard work is the way to success (no pain, no gain right?) but this observation of life is an illusion.

When I was 16 years old I worked in a supermarket stacking shelves and just like everyone else who worked there, I hated my job! At the start of the working day I would stand in a queue with all of my colleagues who worked the same shift pattern as me. The queue was for the 'clock in machine', you would take your time card and get it stamped by the machine to confirm what time you had started work. We all started our shift at 8am, there was really no need for a queue but nobody would 'clock in' until exactly 8am. Not a single person ever pushed a card in that machine at 7.58 or 7.59 and nobody ever 'clocked out' before 5pm exactly. You see, they didn't start paying you until 8am and the mentality of the staff was that they didn't want to work even one second for free. They hated the job so much that they couldn't bear the thought that they had done anything for free.

Sure you could say that all the people working in that supermarket were 'working hard'. I am sure that come Friday night they are exhausted and really ready for a weekend off. But I will tell you that virtually all of that tiredness comes from swimming up the river, kicking like hell to get away from scarcity. Since I quit the 9 to 5 rat race I don't consider that I work hard by the traditional definition. My father (a man that subscribes to the hard work principle of life) would look at my life and say 'you are a bloody lucky sod, you are basically retired at 40 years old). I don't work hard and I don't turn up at an office for forty hours a week, but somehow I still pay my bills, support my children and live in a villa in the Cyprus sunshine. Some days I don't do anything 'worky', I just grab the surfboard and go to the beach. Other days we fire up the BBQ and sit in the sunshine drinking lemonade all day. But when I do work I am like a machine, I achieve more in a day than I used to do in a month back when I was an employee doing a job I was bored with.

As I sit here writing this chapter, it's 4am. I woke up with the urge to write and as I sit here, the words flowing from my fingers, I love every second of it. I feel such passion, excitement and gratitude, because I know these books are going to enhance the lives of thousands of people. I don't care what time of day it is and I have no expectation of how long I will 'work' for. I may keep typing until the sun comes up or I may close the laptop and go back to bed at the end of the next sentence, but the point is I am doing what I love. Back when I did a job that someone else told me to do, if they had ordered me to start work at 4am I would have gone crazy. I would have kicked and screamed and grumbled my way through the shift, all the time declaring the boss to be an asshole and the company 'ridiculous.' Sitting here in the quiet early hours of the morning writing this book is an act of love. I don't resent being awake at this early hour, I am not worried about what I write and I have no deadline. I have completely let go of the illusion that I am in control of what happens with this book. Of course my ego occasionally chips in with a 'what if nobody buys it' or 'what if it is no good' and I respond immediately by saying to myself 'so what if it is junk, I enjoyed writing it' or 'whether this book is designed to help other people or just me, it makes no difference to the love I put into it'.

But why is there such power in letting go, how can 'nothing' be the secret to manifesting a life that you love?

The answer to this question is where I take the biggest risk in our relationship together. I am taking a leap of faith here and I am explaining this to you because I believe we are kindred spirits. You have found this book for a reason and if you are this far in then I am assuming you don't hate it enough to have thrown it in the trash and stormed back to the bookstore to complain. In my book 'The Fragment of God' I explain that the biggest illusion we have to overcome is that of separation. We believe that we are unique and separate from the earth because unlike a tree we are not rooted to the spot, we are free to move independently around our planet and sometimes even off it!

If somebody hurts us we assume that an external force interfered with our life and we label that person 'bad' or even 'evil'. We take this illusion even further by stating that there is a supreme being that we call God, but this deity resides in the heavens and looks down on us. Some religions portray God as all loving, some say he is angry, tempestuous and judging us. I am not here to pass comment on any particular religion and for the purposes of this book it doesn't matter whether you are Christian, Catholic, Jewish, Atheist or Agnostic. Like I said this action of the universe is a law, it doesn't care whether you believe or not and it won't stop working just because you refuse to believe. In exactly the same way that I won't shoot off into space no matter how much I deny the law of gravity.

There is no separation, from anything or anyone. We are one and the same, and this can be easily proved by science of all things. Under an electron microscope we are all comprised of the same material, I don't just mean human beings, I mean everything. People, animals, the earth, the sea, everything is made of tiny subatomic particles of energy vibrating at a specific frequency. Insisting that we are separate from each other is similar to taking a cup of water out of the ocean and saying 'this water is no longer the ocean'. You may be the correct in that a cup of water cannot be 'labeled' as an ocean but it's quite clear that the separation is only a temporary illusion. As soon as you pour the water back into the sea it once again becomes the ocean, but the question is; did it ever stop being the ocean?

In reality, we are not separate from anything. Our earthly bodies simply create the illusion of individuality. To give you a childish example of what I mean; imagine you have a large ball of modeling clay. You pull a chunk of the material from the ball and make a little figurine of a solider. You keep repeating the process until all the clay is used up and you have two armies of toy soldiers in front of you. In a mock battle played out on your modeling table, army A destroys army B. This is the illusion of separation; in reality of course all the soldiers were essentially the same piece of clay. There are no winners or losers of this battle because at the end of the game you scrunch both armies back into one large ball of clay again, ready for a new adventure but in a different form.

Once you buy this principle it miraculously changes your view of everything in the world. There can be no such thing as strangers; we are as one, connected to all others and they in turn to us. If there were a physical or visible connection rather than just a subconscious one and we directly felt the pain we inflicted on others, how different a place would the world be? It's easy to see that fear-based beliefs such as racism could not exist at all, but also when you pause and consider it further you realize that traditional religion would also cease to be.

If a physical connection would make the world a better place, why didn't God create us with one?

Don't you see that is the whole point of life! In spirit our souls are all interconnected as one, there is no separation. Everyone is equal, nobody is better or worse, weaker or stronger, richer or poorer; we are everything and know everything. Our existence is perfect; we can't experience anything but pure love because we inhabit an environment where negative behavior can't possibly exist. All acts are committed against ourselves and we are acutely aware of that. Hatred, jealously and aggression are instantly rendered redundant by our oneness.

Since the big bang the universe has been expanding rapidly and will continue to do so until it reaches critical mass and at that point it will begin to reverse and contract in on itself. From this time onward everything we know will shrink and compress until we arrive back at a state just before the big bang, a position of pure zero. This is not the end but rather this is the beginning of a new cycle. Exactly the same as we are born and later die, the universe, as we know it will also eventually die and then is re-born in a new form created by an entirely new big bang. Our physical and spiritual energy is a part of the universe; because we are not separate from it we must do exactly the same as the host. Our divine purpose is to grow and expand at the exact same pace as the universe as a whole. Without the ability to experience life in physical form this is not possible. Essentially we cannot grow in spiritual form because we have already achieved perfection. We know that we are God and there is literally no place left for us to go.

As strange as it sounds, our souls existing in that permanent state of perfection become sterile. We can't grow or continue our desire to expand because we have already achieved everything. For want of a better analogy 'you really can get too much of a good thing'. The only possible way to appreciate something is to be aware of what it feels like to have the opposite. To appreciate love you must be able to compare it to hate. To be aware of what it feels like to be happy you must also know despair. Without this point of comparison the emotions we enjoy so much become valueless. Ultimately, for God to experience himself as a God he must view himself from our earthly point of view. We come to earth deliberately separated from our brothers and sisters so we can experience the physical contrast of life. This is why murder, crime, illness, natural disasters and all other human suffering exist and why our prayers appear to fall on deaf or uncaring ears. It's not that God wants us to suffer, but rather he wants us to remember who we are. Without the point of reference that suffering provides, joy and love cannot be appreciated and we cannot experience growth.

To give you an example, consider how you feel about the simple act of breathing in and out. We don't have any particularly strong emotions connected to the continuous act of absorbing oxygen and expelling carbon dioxide. We don't appreciate its importance until we are made to try and experience life without it. As a child when you first experienced swimming in water, despite how easy it looked you will never forget that feeling of panic when you felt your head quickly disappearing beneath the surface. Your muscles quickly depleted the oxygen in your blood forcing you to instinctively open your mouth to take in a fresh load of air. Suddenly you became aware of the terrifying sensation of water and not air entering your gasping lungs. A sense of blind panic spreads rapidly from your chest, through your entire torso and out to your thrashing limbs. In that moment, how much did you appreciate the boring every day activity of breathing in and out, and how amazing did the first gasp of life giving air feel as you were scooped out of the water in the arms of your parents?

Here is the most dramatic and sometime problematic statement that I make. We are not just created by God, we are God. I don't mean that I am God or that you are God I mean exactly what I say 'we are God'. Imagine for me that God, the universe, the higher self or whatever you want to call 'it' is that ocean we talked about earlier in the book. Each one of us is that cup of water lifted from the sea… sure it appears that we are not the ocean (or God) when viewed from the context of separation. But in the same way that the cup of water returned to the sea becomes the ocean again and by proxy proves that it never stopped being the ocean, we will eventually realize that the power of divinity always resided within ourselves and not in an external location or at the end of a journey.

If you are religious and have strong beliefs about God please do believe me when I say I am not here to offend or insult your beliefs. For me what religion you are doesn't matter, as long as love is the core principle of what you believe then everything else is just decoration to help a mass audience understand. The objective of this series of books is to show you that there is a divine power operating within you and it is more powerful than you have ever got close to appreciating.

I want you to disregard any image you may have already created to represent God in your mind. To help you do that I am going to ask you to consider one of the most extreme theories of who or what God is. I neither agree nor disagree with the conclusion I am about to describe, but I do find it fascinating to consider the sheer enormity of scale that the scenario suggests.

Start with the premise that our universe is virtually identical to the composition of an atom. The Sun is positioned at the center as its nucleolus and the planets rotate around it, just as electrons do in the smallest element known to man. How big is an atom? Well, if I tell you that in a single grain of sand there are around 500 sextillion atoms then it will give you an idea of how small a thing we are talking about. From our subjective point of view, of being a tiny human being with an extremely large ego we consider ourselves to be pretty damn important. We also look out at the night sky and declare that we live in a truly vast universe. But what if planet Earth, the Sun, Mars, Venus and the Milky Way all just make us one single atom in the REAL universe?

Now consider that in the human body, atoms combine to create cells, the building blocks of life. These cells multiply to form human tissue and organs such as the liver and kidneys. Each cell in the body contains around one hundred trillion atoms and the average human is made up of around seventy trillion cells.

Consider the possibility that God is really a vast life form and everything we know and believe to be real actually represents one trillionth of one cell in the body of this indescribably enormous life. Our entire universe could simply be just a single atom residing within the body of our deity. Stop reading and think about that concept because it blows your mind at the scale and possible size of God.

It's such a dramatic and ultimately improvable theory that it doesn't warrant a great deal of consideration, but it does serve to put your overactive ego back in its place. While at the same time answering some very profound questions:

Where is God?

If we accept for a moment that we are merely a microscopic particle of God's eternal body, the only logical answer to this question is; he is everywhere, you are always connected to him, and essentially you are God.

Did he really create everything?

This is like asking if you created your own liver. Of course the answer is yes, even if you didn't do it consciously. Under this infinite premise God not only created everything, he *is* everything. You are not a separate entity from your liver; it is a part of you.

What is the purpose of life?

In this context, the reason we live is purely to give life to God. We exist so he can exist; it's only our ego that refuses to accept this as the sole point of life, insisting we are more important than we really are. In this theory it also confirms that God loves and cares about us, we are essentially a part of him and he cannot exist without us and vice versa. If God cares for us in the same way that we care for our own cells, you start to see a similar pattern and explanation for the suffering on earth. Every day millions of cells in our body expire only to be instantly replaced by new ones. Do we mourn the loss of those dead cells? Do we get upset that some cells died too young or unfairly? No, of course not; we just let them do what they were designed to do. It is not unfeasible to see God's interaction with us in a similar way.

Could it be that God cares as much for us as we care for our own liver cells? Surely we should all care about our bodies, as they are the only home we will ever have. But perhaps cells are too small for us to really worry about and so we drink, smoke and do all those other things that kill cells by the million. We do this without batting and eyelid, in the same way most people would happily swat a fly dead but the same people are unlikely to pick up a shot gun and take down a dog. It would appear size does matter in certain circumstances! But don't let that tiny prospect lead you to assume you are not a significant cog in the machine, capable of making an impact on the world. If you have ever shared a bedroom with a single mosquito you will understand how significant even the smallest of being can be.

You are going to find that this series of books is more an unlearning process than it is an instruction manual. To achieve happiness, peace and purpose the lists of things to strip away vastly outweigh the list of things to be done. Indeed there is only one state you ever need in your life and that is love. There is nothing else, if your emotions, intentions and deeds are forged from the pure state of love then you are vibrating at the same frequency as the universe itself and nothing but peace, love and abundance will flow into your life. We started by getting rid of the concept of feeling the need to 'do' or to 'kick' (and I will show you how you practice this towards the end of this book), next we understood the illusion of separation, which leads us to drop the belief that we are disconnected from other people. But more than that, to also know that prayers and wishes directed at the external force that many call God are also misdirected. God is not out there somewhere; we ARE God, the power to manifest a joyful life already exists within us. For all these years we have been searching for a treasure map, trying the find the location of the big Red Cross that marks the spot and all the time we were standing on top of it.

In order to achieve peace in life you have to embrace the temporary and stop trying to apply permanency to everything. The secret is to know that there has never been a storm that did not eventually end but equally the heat wave also gives way when the time is right. Both good times and bad times will end and you have accept that this is something that will never change. There will be times in your life when you are wealthy and you will experience times of wanting more. You will have good health and poor but avoid the temptation to declare one of these to be good and the other bad. Neither label is appropriate, accept the ebb and flow of life, always expect things to improve soon.

You cannot fully embrace this principle until you deal with the biggest permanency of all, the event the ego fears more than any other, death! You will struggle to be comfortable with the 'now' if you are terrified of the oblivion you believe is coming to you. You need an exit strategy from this life, this means you need to be relatively clear in your own mind as to what is going to happen when you die. It doesn't really matter what you believe, as long as you believe something. So if you are an atheist and you believe when you die, that's it! Then that's fine, but you have to work on yourself so you can become comfortable with this. If you are worried about falling asleep one day and never waking up again you are going to struggle to find peace in this lifetime. If at the moment you believe death means an eternity of oblivion then you are experiencing fear and fear is always a sign that you are 'kicking'. If you are scared of what being dead feels like, let me ask you this…

Do you remember what it felt like before you were born? Does that lack of knowledge upset or scare you?

If not, then what are you worried about? You have already been to the place you fear the most and it was fine, was It not?

If you are religious and you believe you are destined for heaven, then embrace that and take comfort in your belief. Really, it doesn't matter if you are right or wrong because either way the belief will give you peace in this lifetime, in this moment and that is the only time that will ever exist. I respect your exit strategy, whatever shape it takes and I don't need you to have the same one as me or anyone else – there are no rules. As long as what you believe feels like it is based in love (and not kicking and screaming into oblivion) then you have an exit strategy that works. I will share with you what makes sense to me, my hope is that it resonates with you at a deep level and it adds to your sense of peace.

Firstly and most importantly, there is no such thing as death. You are not really you in the way that you currently believe; this is just the illusion of separation that we talked about earlier. There are not seven billion people on this planet; there is one person in seven billion containers. We place a great deal of focus on our birth and death but only because this is the point where the ego became alive and is the point where that piece of meat in your head will die. From the point of view of who you really are, birth and death are largely irrelevant acts. It would be the same as drawing a cup of water from the ocean and declaring that in doing so the water had now been born. Then when you tip the cup back into the sea the water has died (because it is no longer in the cup). When you look at it from this point of view you realize that birth and death are also a profound illusion. The water existed before it was 'born' and it did not cease to be after you emptied it from the container. If you can embrace the concept that we are just one entity choosing to divide our self into billions of individual fragments. And that in doing so we accelerate our vibration and never ending expansion. Then you will understand that you are not 'you' and I am not 'me' and as such you cannot die because you also exist in me and in every living thing on earth. The day you die you will be replaced by nearly 400,000 new lives. Everyday over 370,000 babies are born into this world, hundreds of thousands of new cups of water drawn out of the ocean and labeled as 'a new life'.

In short, you cannot die. Today hundreds of thousands of new lives started and you are in every single one of them. Right now in this very moment you are being cradled in the arms of your mother in Nigeria, you are being rushed into surgery in New York, you are meeting your grandparents for the first time in London, you are hearing the voice of your father as he holds his pride and joy in Berlin. Once you start seeing everyone as you, then all negative emotion (kicking up stream) becomes pointless. I understand this is a difficult concept to get your head around but at the moment the human race is like the branches of a tree, all living under the illusion that they are separate and different from all the other branches, just because at first glance that appears to be the case. If everyone is you then why would you ever be jealous of your colleague who was promoted ahead of you at work? What would be the point in getting angry with the driver who cut you off on the highway and wouldn't murder, rape and other abuse be the most ridiculous thing you could ever do?

It took me a long time for this penny to drop; if I am being honest it was probably a decade before it started to feel logical. Once the thought becomes a belief then your life really starts to change. When you see the homeless guy begging for something to eat, he is no longer a stranger, instead he appears to be just another version of you, but one that has fallen on hard times. When you hear about children starving in Africa the way you feel about it changes, it becomes more personal. You desperately want to help, to do something to ease their suffering. Can we agree that if everyone treated each other as though they were dealing with themselves that the world would be not just better but heavenly?

This is not a new concept that I have just invented, the theory that we are all the same divine being has been around for as long as time itself. Eastern philosophy dating back thousands of years makes constant reference to this idea and despite the countless wars and acts of terrorism that have been committed in the name of traditional religion, there is a *Golden Rule* in virtually every religious scripture you can think of.

"You shall love your neighbour as yourself. There is no other commandment greater than this." Mark 12:31 – The Golden Rule of Christianity

"Hurt not others in ways that you yourself would find hurtful" The Golden Rule of Buddhism

"This is the sum of duty; do naught onto others what you would not have them do unto you." - The Golden Rule of Hinduism

"No one of you is a believer until he desires for his brother that which he desires for himself."- The Golden Rule of Islam

"What is hateful to you, do not do to your fellowman. This is the entire Law; all the rest is commentary."- The Golden Rule of Judaism

"Regard your neighbour's gain as your gain, and your neighbour's loss as your own loss"- The Golden Rule of Taoism

The fact that this one simple belief is universally shared I find breathtakingly beautiful and reassuring. There are many very famous books on *manifesting the life of your dreams*, *reality creation* and the Law of Attraction in general, the most famous being 'The Secret' by Rhonda Byrne. I am pretty sure you have at least read one of them and I also fairly sure that the results you got were not quite what you were hoping for. There are several reasons for this and the first is that when a book is considered for publishing, the literary agent and publisher are looking for content that will sell in bulk. Often this means that books that don't offend too many people and at least offer concepts that can be tolerated by most everyday people are going to hit the bookshelves rather than books such as this which ask you to make giant leaps of faith and consider that we as a species haven't just got it all 'a little bit wrong' but are on the complete flip side of reality. A lot of the books that made it through the filters ended up being diluted and sanitised to be more palatable to a mass audience and as such they don't deliver much more than you would get from a few weeks deliberate positive thinking. The other reason I don't believe you had the success you really wanted is the very same reason why I have broken this book into parts and I have deliberately got nearly two complete volumes into the series without even mentioning how you start to manifest magic into your life. You must embrace the concept of connectedness before you move on to the next level. If you want a new car because your neighbour just got one then nothing I tell you from here on will work, so you might as well put the book down and save yourself some time and money. If you want a pay rise and promotion because you kind of like the idea of being the head guy at work then the same advice applies.

Before you go any further in this course in miracles try to get this concept into your head. Take a walk around your neighbourhood and watch people going about their day-to-day life; try to imagine that they are all you. As you walk past the homeless guy that you may have ignored for months, see how you feel about him when you imagine that he is you. I want you to see the guy at work who you know stabs you in the back as often as he can, understand why he is doing it… what emotion is he trying to kick away from. What you now know for certain is his behaviour is the direct result of him taking advice from his ego. He is experiencing a 'kicking' emotion such as fear, jealously, resentment or low self-esteem. Forgive him for this behaviour the same way you would explain away your own such actions. I am sure at some point in the past you have acted pretty shabbily towards someone and then justified it with "he deserved it" or "well she shouldn't have started it". This time force yourself to ignore the ego and only act with love, as though you are dealing with yourself on a bad day. It's really easy to skip this exercise and just keep reading but if you want the impact that you dream about then actually spending a few days or a week doing this will make a big difference.

The very exciting news I have for you is by the end of this short book you will know how to start manifesting the life of your dreams. I will give you practical instructions on how you can grant your own wishes. Whether you want more money, better relationships, spiritual peace, better health, security for your family it is all possible. Before we get to that well kept secret of the universe (and no skipping forward please) I did promise you earlier in the book that I would help you deal with those 'kicking emotions'. The single biggest obstacle to you attracting the life of your dreams is the ego and these thoughts and feelings that I refer to as 'kicking emotions'. The reason why this happens is down to the way the mind tries to cope with the limitations of the conscious mind. The ego driven conscious is the poor cousin of the subconscious and can only process one or two tasks at a time. This is why as a child somebody, at some point challenged you to rub your belly and pat your head at the same time and you found it difficult to do.

The subconscious is like a NASA super computer and the conscious is a pocket calculator in comparison, anything more complicated than one or two actions at a time must be passed to the subconscious for completion. To give you an idea of just how out gunned the ego is in this respect. Let me tell you that the human face contains 46 individual muscles. In order to complete the seemingly simply task of a smile, the subconscious must simultaneously activate and control 26 of those muscles in a very specific pattern to create the positive facial expression we call a smile. If this same task were left to the conscious mind it would be nothing short of a shambles. This part of the brain could only hope to activate each muscle in a series rather than parallel. One muscle at time, the result would be a facial expression similar to that of a stroke victim.

The subconscious is aware of this weakness and tries to help out by building physical neural pathways to complete tasks that you do often. There is actual tissue created in your brain to facilitate routines that you run on a regular basis. Because the mind cannot tell the difference between reality and vividly imagined events it gets fooled into creating pathways for thoughts. If you think you are fat and ugly often enough the subconscious will basically assume that the conscious can be spared the effort of constantly thinking this by the subconscious turning it into a permanently stored belief, thus freeing up runtime for the conscious mind to perform other tasks. The biggest problem when this happens is that the subconscious and the soul are one and the same, as such you are inadvertently ensuring that you never become happy with your body and never feel the self-confidence in your appearance that you truly desire. It doesn't matter how many positive mantras you say or how many times you attempt to use the law of attraction to get the body you desire, it will never arrive as long as this broken program keeps running in your unthinking mind. We must stop responding to 'kicking emotions' such as hate, jealousy, resentment and low self esteem to prevent them being passed to the soul to complete automatically.

This function of the brain reminds me of a very funny (and at times painfully sad) movie starring Adam Sandler called 'Click'. In which an ambitious architect called Michael Newman, played by Sandler makes a deal with the Devil, whereby he is given a universal remote control that not only does all the usual things you would expect from such a device such as turning on the television or opening the garage doors but in addition it can also magically control real life too. Michael quickly realises to his delight that with the click of a button he can fast forward through time and even skip events all together. He stumbles across this apparently miraculous feature of the remote while shivering in sub zero temperatures waiting for his dog to take a leak before bed. The pooch is quite happy sniffing around the yard, oblivious to the encouragement to 'do his business' coming from his frustrated and freezing owner. Curiously Newman points the remote at the dog and hits the fast forward button. In a blur of activity including the rather repugnant cocking of the leg incident he is left gobsmacked by the awesome power of his new device.

As the story unfolds he uses the remote more and more, skipping arguments with his wife, fast forwarding boring visits from the in-laws and eventually incorrectly assuming he was shortly to be promoted at work he asks the remote to jump forward to the day he makes partner at his firm of architects. What he doesn't realise is his promotion was actually a whole decade away and the remote is an intelligent device that learns the behaviour of its owner and then attempts to predict the future. The remote assumes that because he has skipped such things as sex with his wife, play time with his kids, Christmas and birthday parties that in the future he will also not want to experience them. It then proceeds to ignore his objections and automatically fast forward him through some of the most sacred and special moments in life. Towards the end of the movie we see an aged, ill and overweight Michael Newman who is distraught because he has missed his children growing up, lost his wife to another man and has sold his soul to be the most successful partner in the company. He is desperately unhappy and full of regret at throwing away all the moments that makes life really worth living.

In book one of Manifesting Magic I asked you to spend a few weeks just becoming aware of the ego speaking. Noticing those kicking emotions playing out in your day-to-day life. I hope you did the exercise because it will make the next part of this course a lot easier to do. Before you start trying to change the parts of your life that you don't want and instead start manifesting more of the elements you do want I want you to spend a few weeks deliberately countering the 'kicking emotions'. This is simple to do and just requires a little dedication and commitment from you. The next time you experience any negative thought or emotion I want you to be aware that it is pushing you away from your goal and to make a statement either verbally or just silently in your head, that puts a positive or loving spin on the situation.

Example One: *Your boss criticizes your work.*

The ego will respond by telling you what a jerk this guy is and anyway how would he know what 'good work' looks like? He doesn't get into the office until 10am and is gone by lunch.

As you become aware of this 'kicking' response, force yourself to come up with a positive and or loving reaction to what has happened. You might say 'wow he must be under a lot of pressure, I hope he is ok' or 'perhaps he is right, maybe I could have pushed a little harder on this project – next time I will nail it for him'.

Example Two: Your daughter still hasn't tidied her bedroom like she promised she would!

The ego will suggest that she is being lazy or is disrespecting you. Again catch yourself in the middle of 'kicking' and instead of doing what you would usually do, put a positive spin on it. Assure yourself that she is just being a teenager and she will soon get better and more considerate.

If these suggestions are making you frown then first be aware that this assessment and scepticism is in itself an act of 'kicking' and secondly remember the concept that separation is an illusion. Would you be so quick to label yourself a jerk for correcting someone else's work? Back when you were a child did you always do what was asked of you the instant it was asked, or did you procrastinate sometimes?

Expect to have to put some effort into this, it is likely you have spent a lifetime listening to the voice of your ego and kicking like crazy to get up the river. Sometimes you will forget to correct yourself and sometimes you will be so angry that finding something good to say will seem impossible. This is why I ask you to do this for a few weeks, at least 21 days so it can start to become a habit rather than something you have to concentrate very hard on to achieve. Only when you have made some progress in this area should you move on to the next section, actually manifesting your wishes into reality. I know you are probably just going to skip ahead, whose curiosity is so well behaved that it will sit quietly by when there are wishes waiting to be granted, right? But seriously, if you start trying to manifest before you get a handle on this kicking behaviour you will be wasting your time, lowering your expectations and in the worst case bringing forth into your life the exact opposite of what you desire.

For example if you try to manifest more money while you still have the conditioned response that money is only for 'greedy' people you will just keep pushing financial abundance further away from you.

Try to think of your subconscious as the most perfect, fertile garden the world has ever seen. The soil is rich and completely free from stones. It contains an abundance of nutrients to grow whatever you plant quickly and lushly. But all that is irrelevant if you plant weeds. There is no filter to this garden; it will grow whatever you sow. If you plant the thing you don't want then that is what you will get more of.

To start manifesting what you desire into your life the process is simple, but only when you have the foundations we have talked about so far. By the way it doesn't matter how you label this process. Some call it wishing, goal setting, manifesting, reality creation and of course the most traditional praying. Many non-religious people sometimes refuse to call it praying but it really doesn't matter what you call it and getting hung up on the label is just as much a 'kicking emotion' as any other. Call it what makes you feel most comfortable.

As a whole, we seem to have got terribly mixed up about praying. More often than not we only drop to our knees and ask God for help only in our darkest moments. We see prayer as a cry for help, like a child who has fallen off the swing screams for his mother. What upsets us with prayer is when we fall off the swing and 'mom' doesn't come running. Our cries for help appear to go unnoticed, and this causes us a great sensation of being alone and unloved.

When traumatic events happen to us we ask what we believe to be entirely reasonable things of a God, who is supposed to care beyond all others. In the darkest of moments we beg that God makes the cancer go away or grants us just enough luck to keep the business afloat for just another week. Whatever it is, these prayers are born of desperation and are unlikely to result in the outcome we desire. When the family member dies and the business goes under we feel abandoned by God. We look to the heavens and wonder why he chose to ignore us in our darkest moment. We want to ask why our prayer wasn't answered but are faced with nothing but silence.

The reality is every prayer is answered, it's just that sometimes the answer is no and at other times it is a qualified yes, 'as in not now but later'. When most people drop to their knees and ask God for something and they don't get the response they want, they make the assumption that God either did not hear, chose to ignore the prayer, or worse still, that God does not even exist.

I am hoping that you can now see that the traditional view of God sitting on a glorious and opulent throne in the heavens is childish nonsense. God is not a person and as such cannot be accused of displaying any sort of human behavior. God did not ignore the prayer or choose to let the individual suffer. The very suggestion of such actions insinuates that we are back at image of a vengeful deity who is separate from us. A God who sits in judgment of our sins on earth, handing out rewards and punishment accordingly.

We must keep reminding ourselves that both time and the illusion of separation are not real. God exists within you; he is embedded inside you as that fragment we talked about earlier.

If you are God and God is you… then where do you think your prayers should be addressed?

That's right you have the power to grant your own prayers. That does not mean you can decide to win the lottery tomorrow or go around healing the sick. Remember all these desires to own things, be more successful, achieve greater wealth and be faster, bigger, slimmer or better than other people are just the insane ramblings of your ego. Do you not think that the divine part of you can tell the source of these material demands and chose to ignore them in your best interests? Equally do you really have to doubt whether the fragment of God within you knows what is best for you, even before you ask?

Your soul not only knows what is best for you but it wants to give it to you. A lifetime of blissful happiness is lined up for you, if you would just let go of the illusion that you are in control of life. For most of your time on this earth you have struggled to swim upstream, determined to get to something you have decided you need to be happy. I am here to tell you that if you just stop kicking and struggling then all you could ever need is waiting for you down stream, where the river wants to take you.

Most people don't really understand the power of prayer. But that's ok because as you would expect its far more simple to do than you might expect. Riding a bicycle is easy if you know how to do it, right? But when you first try to get on one and ride, did you not fall flat on your face? Initially you could stay on that thing for more than a couple of seconds before tumbling off and collecting a few cuts and bruises on the way. Eventually your dad probably fitted training wheels to that bike so you wouldn't get discouraged. Once your confidence had grown and more importantly you believed you could really ride the bike, he took the stabilizers off and set you on your way with a helping push.

Manifesting through prayer is no different; it is a simple thing to do when you know how. The difference is, hardly anyone stops you when you are getting it wrong and puts your training wheels on for a while.

When most people pray for something they kneel, close their eyes and direct their thoughts upwards to the heavens. They say something like "*God, please help me pay the bills this month, we work very hard and when payday comes there is still not enough money to makes ends meet. Make this month better than last month and allow something to happen so we have enough to get by. If you can do that for me I promise I will come to church more often / give to charity more / be a better person*" etc, etc.

A month later and the bills remain unpaid, the person feels his prayer was ignored and then the ego kicks in again with the usual nonsense of 'God must be punishing me'. Why do we find it easier to assume that God is angry with us than that he didn't hear it in the first place? In reality, that person answered their own prayer, but they didn't get the outcome they wanted because they placed the request in the future. This person stated that the present moment is bad and the future will be better. Only the ego operates in the past and in the future; the soul and God work only in the present.

You can tell when you are communicating with the ego because of the positioning in time of the statements. If you are talking about what went before or speculating about what will happen in the future, the conscious mind is active and the subconscious is disengaged. All promises are statements of the ego, even the ones that appear to be well-intentioned. Many state marriage as the counter argument to this, stating that in this moment of loving union God requires us to make promises of fidelity and commitment to each other.

God did not write the marriage vows, a human did. God requires nothing of you beyond what you are right now in this moment. Marriage, like every other decision, will either serve you or it won't, but don't be under any illusion that those publically made statements are anything other than the ego attempting to control the uncontrollable by predicting the future.

Please don't misunderstand; I am not out to do marriage down, but I believe whilst some get a great deal out of marriage and evolve as a soul because of the lessons learnt during the process of sharing a life. Many, many more individuals slowly become resentful and unhappy trying to comply with the needs and desires of another.

If we come to earth as physical beings in order to experience life as a separate entity, why would the logical goal be to settle down with another? The ego is a huge fan of marriage because it simply adores statements that make promises based on 'forever more'. Your soul knows how you feel about your partner in life right now in this moment, but it will never try to predict that you will feel the same in ten years' time, next week or even in the next minute. Only the ego tries to make predictions of the future based on events of the past, and for that reason all promises are simply statements of the ego.

As you stand at the altar and look into your husband's eyes and promise to love him for the rest of time, you are writing promises your soul can't cash. Who knows how you will feel in a week's time, never mind a lifetime? On your ruby wedding anniversary you may be just as head over heels in love as you were on your wedding day, or you may be desperately unhappy. It's impossible to know, but that doesn't stop your ego from trying to convince you it does know.

Any prayers set in the future are destined to fail because it is only a statement of the ego and nothing more. Prayers are answered by your soul, the fragment of God operating in blissful ignorance of the past and future. Ask your soul for a lottery win this weekend and you will get nothing in return. This weekend does not exist in the eyes of your soul. The only thing that exists from the point of view of God is this precise moment. To become a creator of your destiny rather than someone who reacts to the life that has been forced upon them, you need to see the beauty in every moment and be grateful for it.

Think about this moment now, what is amazing in your life now? If your automatic answer is 'nothing, my life sucks at the moment', you are not trying hard enough. Spend a few moments thinking about what is really special in your life now.

Let me give you an example of how you can choose to focus on the negative and make your prayers based on that. At the moment I know that I feel sad because I don't get to see my family enough, because my work takes me around the world. I feel a little guilty that I don't get to be the hands on father that I dreamt I would be because I am away on business so often. I know there is big tax demand on the way and I am not looking forward to paying that... I could go on and on. Then I could drop to my knees and say *'God, please let me spend more time with my family and help me pay the tax demand'* etc, etc. This prayer will not work, or perhaps more accurately I should say, this prayer would not give me the outcome I desire.

All that prayer will deliver is more of what I have focused on in the moment that I offered it. In that precise moment I had 'sadness', 'guilt' and 'worry' on offer, and that is exactly what I will get more of as a result. Your soul is a divine creator, a manifestation weapon of limitless power, but with the safety switch off... be careful where you point that thing, it might go off! Aim it at the negative and it will create more negatives (free will is a pain, right?), but aim it at the positive and guess what happens?

So, let's talk about me again (my ego will love this), but instead of thinking about the lack of time I got to spend at home last month, or that big bill that is coming next month, let's stay in this precise moment and build a prayer based on that.

Right now I am so grateful that I am sharing this knowledge with you, I know that these words resonate with me at a very deep level and I am excited about the impact they might make to kindred spirits around the world. I have two stunningly amazing children who I love with all my heart. I have someone special in my life that loves me very much. I have food, shelter, safety and all the other basic requirements of life. It's 7.15am and I am sitting at my desk listening to the soft summer rain outside, today is a blank canvas and I am grateful for the world of opportunities available to me.

Wow, suddenly I feel good… I really encourage you to do the same task, and do it now. Don't let your ego make a promise that you will do this later, grab a piece of paper and start writing now. Scribble down all the amazing things in your life, ignore the stuff that has gone before and avoid the shoulda, woulda, coulda's.

As we have already discovered; your conscious desires and wants are an irrelevance, so forget about what you think you want. These dreams are all in the tomorrow and none of your business. Concentrate on what is in your life today, this moment, and be grateful for it. Even problems present as an opportunity for love and gratitude. Give your problems to God, ask God to erase them and then give thanks for that.

I think Marelisa Fabrega describes it best in her change blog when she says:

Gratitude means thankfulness, counting your blessings, noticing simple pleasures, and acknowledging everything that you receive. It means learning to live your life as if everything were a miracle, and being aware on a continuous basis of how much you've been given. Gratitude shifts your focus from what your life lacks to the abundance that is already present. In addition, behavioral and psychological research has shown surprising life improvements that can stem from the practice of gratitude. Giving thanks makes people happier and more resilient, it strengthens relationships, it improves health, and it reduces stress.

Two psychologists, Michael McCollough of Southern Methodist University in Dallas, Texas, and Robert Emmons of the University of California at Davis, wrote an article about an experiment they conducted on gratitude and its impact on well-being. The study split several hundred people into three different groups and all of the participants were asked to keep daily diaries. The first group kept a diary of the events that occurred during the day without being told specifically to write about either good or bad things; the second group was told to record their unpleasant experiences; and the last group was instructed to make a daily list of things for which they were grateful. The results of the study indicated that daily gratitude exercises resulted in higher reported levels of alertness, enthusiasm, determination, optimism, and energy. In addition, those in the **gratitude** group experienced less depression and stress, were more likely to help others, exercised more regularly, and made greater progress toward achieving personal goals.

People tend to take for granted the good that is already present in their lives. There's a gratitude exercise that instructs that you should imagine losing some of the things that you take for granted, such as your home, your ability to see or hear, your ability to walk, or anything that currently gives you comfort. Then imagine getting each of these things back, one by one, and consider how grateful you would be for each and every one. In addition, you need to start finding joy in the small things instead of holding out for big achievements—such as getting the promotion, having a comfortable nest egg saved up, getting married, having the baby, and so on–before allowing yourself to feel gratitude and joy.

Another way to use giving thanks to appreciate life more fully is to use gratitude to help you put things in their proper perspective. When things don't go your way, remember that every difficulty carries within it the seeds of an equal or greater benefit. In the face of adversity ask yourself: "What's good about this?", "What can I learn from this?", and "How can I benefit from this?"

Once you become oriented toward looking for things to be grateful for, you will find that you begin to appreciate simple pleasures and things that you previously took for granted. Gratitude should not be just a reaction to getting what you want, but an all-the-time gratitude, the kind where you notice the little things and where you constantly look for the good, even in unpleasant situations. Today, start bringing gratitude to your experiences, instead of waiting for a positive experience in order to feel grateful; in this way, you'll be on your way toward becoming a master of gratitude.

One final concept that many get wrong is this. Once you have asked for something don't ever ask again. Your wish/prayer/request was heard, you don't need to repeat it or remind the universe that you are waiting. As soon as you have stated your intention you must KNOW that the object of your desires is on the way. It may take a day, a week, a year or a lifetime but in your heart, mind and soul you must simply know that nothing can stop it arriving into your life. There is no need to keep requesting it over and over again because the act of asking puts you into a kicking mode. You are coming from a position of scarcity and this is the ego assuming that there is not enough of something in the world and you are being ordered to kick upstream to find more.

Let's get down to the brass tacks of how you ask for what you want. How you ask is again something that is totally your decision. Some people just mentally imagine all the amazing things that would change if they had a certain outcome and then they clearly ask the universe/God/their inner being to deliver it. Other people write down their request, detailing how grateful they are for the wonderful events unfolding into their lives. I have tried to give you a simple and effective way of manifesting at my website. If you go to CraigBeck.com/rocketlauncher/ you will find an online tool called the 'Manifesting Magic Rocket Launcher'. This allows you to type your desire and launch it into the universe for completion. It doesn't matter how you launch your rockets of desire just so long as you have faith in the process you have selected. Whichever method you choose, stick to the seven rules (there are always seven for some reason) and your life will start to dramatically change.

Here are the seven rules of Manifesting Magic:

1. **Decide exactly what you want.**
   Asking for a good day is probably too vague; it doesn't mean you won't have a good day but it may be difficult for you to connect the events of the day with the rocket you launched. Be specific but not restrictive, for example 'Thank you for ten sales a day on my website' is better than 'Thank you for ten sales a day from blonde women who live in California'. Again it doesn't mean the super specific request can't happen it's just that you may take so long for this to manifest into reality that you forgot you even asked for it. Additionally, be sure that the specifics you are applying to the request actually add a benefit for you.

2. **Be sure that it does no harm.**
   If what you want causes any other living thing to suffer in any way then the manifestation will fail. Remember, there is no separation; we are all the same core. If you go after your best friend's wife then this is clearly a 'kicking emotion' and you are asking the universe to hurt itself.

3. **Be certain that your desire is born of a positive emotion.**
   Ask yourself why you want what you want. If you have $500,000 in the bank and you are trying to manifest money – why? For what purpose will it serve and does it come from the start point of 'love'? Wanting a new car to boast to your friends does not fit the rule but striving to raise funds to

make a large anonymous donation to a charity most certainly does.

4. **Ask for what you want.**
   Launch your rockets of desire. Be clear about what you want, how it will make you feel and all the wonderful things that it's manifestation will create in your life and in the lives of all those who share your world.

5. **Assume you already have it, express gratitude for it being in your life (but don't need it to be in your life – you must accept a 'no' if that is what is best for you).**

   It's fine to want more money but you don't need it to be happy. If the universe sees a different path for you that doesn't include money (at the moment) you have to be at peace with this. Do not kick against the decision, know in your heart that you are loved and forces are moving to bring what is best for you into alignment.

6. **Never ask again.**
   Don't get confused with self-help advice that suggests you positively state your desires to yourself every morning. The universe is perfect, are you really suggesting it has poor hearing or an unreliable memory? You only need to ask once and then move into the state of KNOWING that it will arrive.

7. **Forget you ever asked.**
   I appreciate that telling someone to forget something is a bit like asking him or her not to think of a pink elephant. You can't try to forget something without first thinking about it. What I mean is, you should avoid worrying about your rocket. Wondering when it will manifest or how you will know it has started to work are both kicking actions of the ego. If you catch yourself thinking about your request just remind yourself that it is on the way and put it out of your mind.

It really is as simple as that, start each day with the sneaking feeling that the world is out to do you good. KNOW that your rockets have not only hit their target but your dreams are on route. Take it easy and start small, don't demand the earth and then get very disappointed when nothing happens. Remember, a lot of this is counterintuitive to everything you have been taught before. At times you are going to have doubts and that's fine – just recognise them as an 'egoic kick' and stop them in their tracks. You are a Manifesting Magic beginner, a white belt at this business… and exactly like martial arts, you can't expect to get your black belt without many years of diligent practice. I know that if you follow the wisdom in this series of books your life is going to dramatically and positively shift… I don't just know it, I **KNOW** it!

I remind you at this point that Manifesting Magic is a course, a jigsaw puzzle of information if you prefer. You can't complete a puzzle with only half of the pieces and the same is true for the Art of Happiness, Peace & Purpose. The life you really want is a wheel supported by spokes. If any of the spokes are missing then true peace cannot be achieved. For example if you are wealthy but poor of health then life is still a struggle. If you are healthy, wealthy but all your relationships are broken and unfulfilling then very few people would choose to swap places with you. The next spoke for your wheel is added in book 3 when we discover the secrets to amazing relationships. This is not just about finding your soul mate (many readers of this book will already be happily settled down with someone they love) but rather it is about our affiliation with all other people who share our world. Making all those people who surround you feel loved and cherished, its about bringing up healthy, happy and successful children, having amazing friends who always have your best interests at heart, making giant strides in your career and yes also getting a mind-blowingly good loving relationship with the man or woman of your dreams.

Secret 3 – How to Find Your Soul Mate

"We are all a little weird and life's a little weird, and when we find someone whose weirdness is compatible with ours, we join up with them and fall in mutual weirdness and call it love", Author Unknown

I am writing this section of the book 34,000 feet above Texas on a flight to San Francisco. As I look around the cabin at all the huge variety of different people sharing this flight with me I am reminded that I know very little about you, the reader of this book. Sure, I know you want to improve certain aspects of your life and that you are prepared to invest your time and money in reaching that goal. Beyond that I can't be expected to know anything else about you. I don't even know if you are male or female. However, of one thing I am certain and that is that there is a broken relationship in your life right now. This could be demonstrated through friction with your boss at work, with your partner, a sibling or even unresolved resentment towards one or both of your parents.

I write about this subject from bitter experience, for many years I felt the world was against me. My boss was an asshole, the people I worked with were incompetent fools getting their unfair share of the financial rewards and even my loved ones were letting me down in some way. I truly believed that I could rely on nobody but myself, anything else was pure folly. When eventually my marriage failed in 2011 I began a protracted series of short-term romantic relationships. Each one was as dramatic as it was traumatic, each eventually ending in a bitter parting of ways.

With each failed attempt to find my 'soul mate' I would declare the most recently failed relationship to have been doomed from the start because she was 'insane', 'too needy', 'jealous', 'uncaring' or any other myriad of reasons why this person was incapable of giving me the loving relationship that I was desperate to experience.

I hope by now you know that I never write from atop an ivory tower. I am not one of those 'spiritual gurus' who shake their heads at you and disappointingly say 'tut, tut, tut – stop living like that and start being more like me'. Through my books I unfortunately share the knowledge that I have been painfully forced to learn the hard way.

Do something for me; call to mind the relationship in your life that you would most describe as being broken or dysfunctional. A relationship that causes you distress when you really wish it were a loving positive element in your life. Whatever you believe the root cause of the trouble is I can tell you that the source of the problem is actually nowhere near where you think it is. Whether you believe this person is arrogant, nasty, condescending or just plain selfish, the label you apply is nothing but an illusion.

My relationship with my boss Brian (name changed) was unworkable because he was lazy and incompetent and as such I didn't respect him. My relationship with Sarah was never going to work because she didn't really care what I wanted out of life, only what she wanted. Catherine and I were a non-starter because she was just too damn insecure and needy.

All these excuses for failure in my life are illusions that I used to firmly be<u>lie</u>ve. I used them to protect my ego, to point blank refuse to accept responsibility for the rampant disharmony in my life. The reality is this; Brian was no lazier than I was. Sarah was focused as much on her life as I was on my own and me calling Catherine insecure is a bit like a catwalk model suggesting her colleague is too vain.

In Manifesting Magic Part 3 I am going to show you the secret to creating powerfully beautiful relationships in your life. Whether these are professional, personal or even close family. We are going to start this profound journey of awakening at the source of all the trouble, YOU! Whether you want to accept it or not, I am here to tell you that the starting point for all the troubled relationships in your life is YOU!

If you think about it logically… your boss can't really be an asshole because if that were true then everyone would agree on it. But I am sure you are aware of people who actually like the guy, even if you have to go as far away from the workplace as to his family and friends. The true label here is 'your boss is an asshole to you'. This course begs the very reasonable question of why he is.

In **Manifesting Magic Part 3** – I will tell you exactly why you have been singled out for such unfair treatment and more importantly, how you stop if from continuing.

We all have this labelling thing the wrong way around. We see the problem in our broken relationships as faults in the other person that have become increasingly incompatible with our own modus operandi. The hard lesson to learn is that the problems you experience in other people are merely reflections of problems that reside inside you. What I am saying is that the disharmony did not exist within Brian, Sarah or Catherine it was inside me from the very beginning. My relationships merely provided a mirror for the pain inside me.

At this early point in the book I confidently expect to lose a significant proportion of my audience. Depending on how bad the relationship you are thinking of is (or was) and what wholly unacceptable things they put you through. I can completely understand your outrage and offense at the very suggestion that you are somehow to blame for their appalling behaviour.

So, here you have a choice. You can express your rage at the very suggestion – write harsh words about the book wherever possible and never open its creamy white pages again… oh and of course continue on with your broken relationship or perhaps even relationships. Or might I instead persuade you to take a leap of faith and understand that I have already myself swallowed this bitter pill, made peace with it and found that the medicine it provides does actually heal the afflicted.

What I know for certain is that if you continue with me on this journey and implement the difficult paradigm shifts I am about to suggest your life will be enhanced and enriched beyond your wildest imagination.

What you see isn't real

What do you see when you look at me?

Do you see a middle aged man with messy hair, a father of two children, an English guy or maybe somebody's partner? Perhaps I just cut you off on the highway and I am most definitely nothing better than a selfish idiot. Or maybe you just dropped your wallet and I handed it back to you… and I am the nice, friendly man who saved you a lot of heartache and trouble. It doesn't really matter what you see or bel*ie*ve about me, it's all an illusion. I am not who you believe me to be, I am merely a mirror for what is inside you.

Sadly we are all guilty of seeing what we want to see. Take your partner for instance, if you so choose you can go on a mission to find evidence that they don't care about you and don't really love you. As sure as night follows day the supporting material for this type of thinking will pile upon itself until you have a cast iron case to prove your point. I can tell you from experience that this theory is true, but the good news is it also works the other way around. If you go on a mission to find evidence that your partner loves and respects you, the proof will turn up everywhere you look.

But how can this be so, the person remains the same and yet by changing the way *you* think you somehow manage to get a polar opposite answer to your question. The short answer is the world you see before you is not solid. It is a fluid creation of your own construction, what you consider to be reality can morph into anything you so choose. The longer answer, I shall dispense forthwith.

I want you to be very clear about who I am. I am not a guru or a saint, far from it. Just like you I read the words of spiritual teachers such as Eckhart Tolle and Deepak Chopra and marvel at their peace and tranquillity of life. I am one of life's thinkers; this has been as much a curse as it is a blessing. For me I can't accept what I do not understand, I must apply logic and reason to the status quo. Unless I do this, the thought will remain an un-caged beast, free to roam and cause misery and mayhem. Of course, this is an impossible mission because many of life's wonders and challenges must forever remain a mystery, and yet I continue to try first to understand them for myself and then share my hard fought comprehension with the world.

I have always advised people who want to lose weight to avoid 'experts' who are skinny and have always been skinny. Equally I advise you avoid the weight loss advice of your obese GP or other chubby healthcare professionals. If you want to lose a significant amount of weight, go ask someone who has been in your shoes and found a way out of the maze. I am not here to reveal how I have always had perfect loving relationships and to chastise you for having fallen short of my perfect standards. That would all be a fabrication of dramatic proportions. I can't tell you that I have always played the mediator and never the aggressor. I can't tell you I have always approached the significant others in my life with selfless love.

When I decide to sit down and write a book I only do so after I have failed at the subject matter many thousands of times. Before I became an expert in stopping drinking and wrote the book 'Alcohol Lied to Me' I was an expert in failing to quit drinking for over a decade. I spent ten years of my life trying to control my alcohol consumption, until one day I worked out what the secret was. I have since cured over 50,000 people from life limiting alcoholism. I could beat myself up for not getting started on this path sooner but that would be pointless. The countless failures all taught me a lesson and the culmination of these experiences gave me the insight to create something that worked.

So here I am writing a book on creating amazing and loving relationships. Exactly the same as all my other books, I sit here with a wealth of knowledge painfully earned. Yes it's true, I am an expert in how **not** to create loving, powerful relationships **and** that is exactly why you should listen to me. Be assured that there is yin to my yang, just as you can't understand what hot feels like without the comparison of cold to relate it to. I can tell you that without my many failures in life I would not have gained the wisdom to reveal this knowledge to you today.

Whether you want to find the man or woman of your dreams, fix your marriage, heal a family rift, get on better with your boss or just find new friends then you will find the three central concepts of this book will help.

- *Concept 1: What you see isn't real*

- *Concept 2: Life is a boomerang*
- *Concept 3: There is nothing to do but clean*

These three concepts will help… But only if you can suspend any disbelief or cynicism, that may be lurking at the forefront of your consciousness. If you can embrace and act upon the principles of this book then you will see dramatic and positive shifts in all your relationships.

Let's leave the tricky concept that how you see other people is nothing but an illusion to one side for a moment and first deal with human motivation, what makes people act and respond the way that they do. It is easy to look at yourself with rose tinted spectacles, assuming that everything you do is totally reasonable and logical. However, when we look at other people we tend to remove the glasses and start labelling their behaviour (which is often no different from our own) as 'selfish', 'mean', 'nasty' or one of thousands of other negative adjectives. The simple fact is we are all dealing with life the best we can, using the resources we have available to us. It really doesn't matter how much of an asshole your boss appears to be or just how selfish your partner is acting at the moment. Nobody is really out to cause misery for other people for the sake of it. They may hurt and offend people but that is rarely their intention or motivation to act the way they do.

Bullies don't bully because they enjoy hurting people, they are insecure people responding the best way they know how to the fear they feel inside. Your ex didn't cheat on you because they wanted to hurt you but rather they were motivated to do so by an internal dialogue with their own fragile ego. This concept applies to everyone, from the guy who cut you off on the highway this morning to dictators of entire nations. No political leader in history who ever ordered his country to go to war against his or her neighbors (and in doing so ensuring the slaughter of many thousands of innocent lives) did so because he wanted to be evil. All these people acted in the belief that what they were doing was good for their people. Even the sickening acts of mass genocide the world witnessed being committed by Saddam Hussein during his long reign over Iraq took place because as a Sunni Muslim of the strict Baathist party, he believed deviation from the precise interpretation of the Koran was a threat to the people of his country. You can bet your life right to the very end Saddam would have firmly believed everything he had done was for the good of his people.

Even in the case of serial killers, they are not behaving with the goal of being evil. They are responding to pain and doing what they think is right to make it go away. With these heartless destroyers of life you can often argue that blame should really be placed with the parents and not with the individual who committed the crimes. A significant number of the criminally insane that make our front page headlines after committing horrendous acts of abuse, rape and murder were themselves mentally tortured and deprived of love as children. I am most certainly not arguing for unconditional leniency for all convicted offenders, and I appreciate if you or your family has suffered directly as a result of someone like this; the very suggestion of such a thing may be extremely upsetting for you. I am only trying to demonstrate that all judgments of what is good or bad are highly subjective.

If a child who was routinely beaten and never shown a single act of human kindness goes on to live a violent life, inflicting pain and suffering on others, who is ultimately to blame?

Think about the actions of western leaders, last week the British media triumphantly reported that RAF air strikes against ISIS terrorists in Syria had successfully killed hundreds of men. To most people in the West the reported deaths of so many (evil) people are largely considered an irrelevance. The prime minister who effectively ordered their deaths is seen as a man making tough decisions in difficult circumstances. But do you think the families of those killed men talk of the British Prime Minister in the same way? Of course they will consider him to be a calculating, hate filled, evil man. The same man, the same acts and completely polar opposite labels depending on who is viewing the situation.

The simple fact is people are rarely acting in the manner that we choose to label them. The reality is they are simply being motivated to act the way they do by the same two psychological influencers that we are all controlled by. There are only two states of mind that direct all human reaction and they are the emotions of pleasure and pain. Everything we do is an act of moving towards pleasure or moving away from pain. Sadly we will always do significantly more to achieve the latter than the former. Pain is the most powerful motivator of human beings. This explains why so many people who are unhappy with the size of their body will go on a diet long enough to lose a couple of pounds but will not complete the journey to arrive at the size and shape body that would make them happy. I call this process of taking action until the pain stops but failing to persist until arriving at pleasure, the threshold matrix.

The Threshold Matrix

Jenny looks in the mirror and grabs hold of the new roll of fat that has slowly developed around her waist. She sighs and looks forlornly at the wardrobe full of clothes that no longer fit. Her weight and body size is making her miserable, but for the moment the pain is not enough to justify giving up the food she loves and associates with a lifestyle she believes herself worthy of. Her current mental assessment is that living without the fine dining, chocolate, cakes and weekend takeaways will be more unpleasant than how she currently feels about her body.

The next day at work something happens that dramatically changes her opinion, as she steps out of the elevator and makes for her cubical she stops short and waits before turning the corner. She hears her name being mentioned in conversation and cocks her head to one side, listening to what is being said. A new intern is asking one of the sales staff who Jenny Taylor is because he has a package to leave on her desk. The salesman, who is rushing out the door on a client call he is already ten minutes late for, shouts over his shoulder 'cubicle 17, big woman, brown hair'!

Jenny's jaw drops open as she gets slapped around the face by the realization that people describe her as 'the big woman' of the office. In my weight loss book Fat Guy Friday this is what I call a threshold moment. This is a point in time when the pleasure/pain balance gets dramatically shifted. Suddenly the pain of being overweight and the associated low self-image becomes massively exaggerated and overtakes the other now insignificant pressure preventing the person from taking action.

Horrified by what she has just overheard, Jenny throws her fried chicken lunch in the garbage and the diet starts immediately. On the way home from work she stops off at the gym and signs up for a yearlong commitment to the dreaded treadmill (despite the fact that she hates the gym, but not quite enough to silence that statement 'big woman, brown hair'). Fitness centres tie you into fixed term deals because they know your current good intentions are going to last six to eight weeks at best. Then you will be banging on their door demanding that they stop debiting your account every month. Regular gym goers hate January because the treadmills and stationary bikes are clogged up with the New Years Resolution gang; thankfully by March most of them are gone. Although chances are good that they are still paying the club fees because ending a gym membership can sometimes be harder than getting a divorce.

The rabbit food replaces the pizza and Jenny Taylor drags herself to the gym daily for a whole month. That salesman gets at least a dozen evil looks a day as the echo of his description bounces around her wounded mind. Diet cereal for breakfast, salad for lunch and boiled fish for dinner… until one day the jeans that were once too tight slide over her hips. A delightful occasion for any dieter and the next day at work, back in her skinny clothes a few of her colleagues notice the weight loss and make pleasing noises in her direction. The motivational scales take another swing as the pain from the threshold moment dissipates and loses it leverage.

Within a week or so Jenny is allowing herself the 'occasional treat' and skipping the gym on days when she feels a little tired. Within a month she has started to resent the $70 a month the fitness centre takes out of her account, as it feels it is poor value for the odd time she actually makes it past the highway turnoff. It's not long before the pain of depriving herself of life's luxuries far outweighs the trauma of that now distant threshold event. The weight slowly returns until the cycle starts again.

This is what we call the yo-yo diet routine and it's why 95% people who go on a low fat, calorie restrictive diet not only put back on any weight lost, but also adds on average an additional 2-5 lbs. Slim folk can look at these people and give them any number of negative labels from lazy to greedy but the truth is they are only doing what we all do – trying to move away from a painful emotion.

So let's take this principle and apply it to the relationships in your life. Take a moment to think about that certain person who you are having trouble with at the moment. It doesn't matter whether it's your teenage daughter who is running amuck, your partner who doesn't seem to be showing you the love and respect you need at the moment or your boss who is making life much more difficult that it really needs to be. As you think about them consider what labels you have chosen to give them in the past. Perhaps you have described your daughter as disobedient, your partner as selfish or your boss as power mad. Close your eyes and try to imagine that you can step outside your own body and be a third party observing your relationship. Cast your mind back to particular fractious time with this individual and imagine you can float above the incident and watch how you and the other person are responding and reacting to each other.

Next leave the labels to one side and try to see what is motivating the other person to be the way they are. Remember that this is easier than it first appears because there are only two motivating forces – pleasure and pain. If your daughter is shouting at you and refusing point blank to tidy her room, consider if she appears to be enjoying the exchange with you. Probably not, and so we must assume she therefore must be being motivated by pain. Perhaps she is struggling with her identity, she doesn't know who she is and what she is supposed to stand for. This confusion mixed with a whole heap of teenage hormones is causing her pain and her only objective is to move away from feeling like this. So she is lashing out you and challenging your authority. Whether she is making the right choice in this moment is irrelevant to the exercise. What you can be sure of is that she is not fighting with you for the sake of it or because she wants to hurt you. She is doing what she believes is the best way to push herself away from pain. She may be incorrect but ask yourself if you have ever won an argument by telling the other person they are wrong.

Remember, we are all doing the best we can with the resources we have. This doesn't mean we should be capable of always making good decisions it just means that most of us are simply dealing with the challenges of life in the way that feels best in any given moment.

Once you can detach yourself from the labels and judgements of your ego. Once you can stop trying to drag your relationship up the river and let go then you will start to see much less drama and stress appearing in your life. Remember, your ego fears loss more than anything else. This doesn't have to be just the thought of losing material possessions but also emotional loss including but not limited to states of mind it believed you owned. If you are a parent you probably believe that you deserve the respect of your child, which may well be true. But the problem is your ego gets attached to that belief and when your child disrespects you they wound your ego by stealing something that you deem to be yours.

STOP RIGHT THERE CRAIG!

Are you seriously suggesting that I should let everyone treat me any way they want?

That I don't even have the right to stand up for myself?

Of course not, there will always be times when you need to act to protect yourself and your family. What I am saying is that 'information is power', if you can detach yourself from responding to the wounding of the ego then you are going to find that life throws significantly less stress and conflict in your direction.

This is what I call mental Judo…

A 10-year-old boy decided to study judo despite the fact that he had lost his left arm in a devastating car accident.

The boy began lessons with an old Japanese judo master. The boy was doing well, so he couldn't understand why, after three months of training the master had taught him only one move. "Sensei,"(Teacher in Japanese) the boy finally said, "Shouldn't I be learning more moves?" "This is the only move you know, but this is the only move you'll ever need to know," the sensei replied.

Not quite understanding, but believing in his teacher, the boy kept training. Several months later, the sensei took the boy to his first tournament. Surprising himself, the boy easily won his first two matches. The third match proved to be more difficult, but after some time, his opponent became impatient and charged; the boy deftly used his one move to win the match. Still amazed by his success, the boy was now in the finals.

This time, his opponent was bigger, stronger, and more experienced. For a while, the boy appeared to be overmatched. Concerned that the boy might get hurt, the referee called a time-out. He was about to stop the match when the sensei intervened. "No," the sensei insisted, "Let him continue." Soon after the match resumed, his opponent made a critical mistake: he dropped his guard. Instantly, the boy used his move to pin him. The boy had won the match and the tournament.

He was the champion. On the way home, the boy and sensei reviewed every move in each and every match. Then the boy summoned the courage to ask what was really on his mind

"Sensei, how did I win the tournament with only one move?"

"You won for two reasons," the sensei answered. "First, you've almost mastered one of the most difficult throws in all of judo. And second, the only known defense for that move is for your opponent to grab your left arm."

The boy's biggest weakness had become his biggest strength.

Mental Judo is a way of dealing with people by using their own force against them. When you are dealing with conflict the other person is normally in a very conscious state of listening to their ego. Whether you are aware of it or not you are causing them pain, their ego is screaming blue murder because you are attempting to steal something from them. Your husband may feel he is having his freedom stolen from him because you want him to spend the weekend with your family instead of playing golf with his friends. Your wife may feel like you have stolen respect from her because you don't appreciate the tough week at work she had. By detaching yourself from responding in kind from your own ego you diffuse the conflict.

Of course this passive approach may mean you have less conflict in your life but the danger is that you fail to get your own needs met. To guard against this, effective communication and establishing clear boundaries is essential. You must be able to express how you feel to the other person (without aggression or attachment to states of mind) and make it clear where your boundaries are. For example your teenage son may not want to tidy his room and he may scream and shout at you. In the past you may have shouted back and responded to his abuse by 'defending' your position as his parent. With mental judo you don't need to attack back because you understand the offending behaviour is not personal, he is just responding to pain. However, that doesn't mean you need to give in to his objections. You can clearly and calmly state where your boundaries are. Nobody has permission to break your boundaries – these are personal and an essential element of your morality.

Summary: Principle one of manifesting magical relationships is to realise why people react the way they do and perhaps so counter to the way you would react in that situation. No matter what the 'other person' has done or said it is not personal. Remember, we are all dealing with life the best we can with the resources we have.

Life is one big boomerang

"You get what you want while you are busy giving other people what they want", Zig Ziglar

The second principle of manifesting magic relationships to understand that life is a mirror. We briefly referred to this early in the book but I want to expand on it a little further before we move onto the third and final principle.

When I first moved to the island of Cyprus I couldn't believe how rude and impolite the Greek Cypriots were. I couldn't even drive to the supermarket without getting cut off on the highway or being aggressively tailgated all the way to the store. People were constantly cutting in line and the people serving me in stores would never smile or offer any politeness. For quite a while I firmly held the belief that the Cypriots were a very rude bunch of people indeed. Then I made a couple of friends who were born and bred in Cyprus. I became good friends with the owner of the local pharmacy, a very wise and friendly guy called Savvas. Shortly after meeting him he took me out to lunch and for three hours we shared good food and conversation. For most of the time he sang the praises of Cyprus and it's people. He told me that I was a very lucky guy because I had the good fortune to live in Cyprus, home to very loving and compassionate people. Savvas insisted that I could spend the rest of my days travelling the world and I would never find more caring people than the Cypriots. Of course I didn't challenge his beliefs, but let's just say I wasn't entirely on board with what he was saying.

But then something strange happened. Over the next few weeks I noticed a dramatic change in the Cypriots. They became better drivers, shop assistants started smiling, strangers in the street started to wish me a good morning as I walked passed them. There are only two explanations for this paradigm shift, either the whole country of Cyprus had a secret meeting and agreed to be a bit more hospitable or more likely the change I was witnessing wasn't out there but rather it was inside me.

Life is a big boomerang, be careful what you throw out there because it's all coming back to you and at speed. This principle is so important that I refer to it as a law. What I mean by this is, it doesn't matter whether you agree with it or not – it's going to happen regardless of your views. In the same way that the law of gravity doesn't care whether you believe in it or not.

I have a friend on Facebook who if I cut and paste all her status updates here for you to read you would think 'the poor girl, what a terrible life she has'. At first glance I would admit she does appear to have extraordinary bad luck but when you take into consideration the boomerang law it all becomes entirely understandable and entirely predictable. If she has to visit the doctor her status will be along the lines of "Wish me luck I am going back to the doctor this afternoon. It will be just my luck that the test results are not even ready yet LOL". Can you guess what her next status update says? I will give you a clue, delete the LOL and replace it with FFS and you will be getting close to the theme of the status.

If you expect the doctor to mess up your consultation you send a manifestation rocket into the universe that this is what you want. If you concentrate on how crappy your marriage is and what a terrible wife or husband you have, can you see how that becomes more and more the reality. Rarely do you wake up and suddenly your marriage is fine again. We have a machine in our head with the power of creation, it's like a manifestation ray gun and whatever you point it at comes into your life. Point it at misery and it traps a load of miserable events in its tractor beam and drags them all closer to you. Point the gun at success or happiness and your life changes in the very best way. So we are all given at birth this magical weapon but it comes with no instruction manual and no safety switch. When you point it at the bad stuff it doesn't say 'are you sure master?' and ask you to click 'ok' or 'cancel'.

So here is a question for you… what happens if you point your ray gun at nothing?

You might leap to the conclusion that nothing happens but that is not quite right. Remember this ray gun gives you more of what its beam focuses on. The nothingness in the spotlight actually expands and grows. It turns a small cavity into a giant chasm and this is what Nazi concentration camp survivor Victor Frankl refers to as the existential vacuum or to give it a less fancy name 'human emptiness'. When we create this void inside ourselves it causes us pain and misery. So we try to fill the hole with stuff, anything that will take away the emptiness. How many people do you know seem obsessed with having luxury in their lives? They want an expensive car to impress the neighbors; they take grand vacations and tell all their friends about how amazing it was, they want a bigger house, designer clothes and all the visible trappings of success that the world can offer. This is all stuff they are desperately trying to plug the emptiness inside with.

Throwing possessions and 'stuff' into the void doesn't make any difference because the ray gun is still pointed firmly at nothing and the black hole keeps expanding and expanding. Acquiring 'stuff' is the strategy for happiness that is likely to be as effective as trying to fill a volcano by throwing in one grain of sand a day. Other people try to close the chasm inside themselves with drugs, alcohol and sex. They become obsessed with either one of these pursuits or sometimes all of them and more, all in the incorrect belief that these things and stuff can stop the pain. How many Hollywood actors and rock stars have you heard of that appear to have the whole world on a plate and yet they end up killing themselves either by suicide, drugs or a combination of the two? But how can this happen in lives that are apparently so full? There probably isn't an answer that can be applied to all situations. Everyone comes into the world with his or her own mission, their own raison d'etre and failing to hit the mark will create an equally unique vacuum.

When you stick in a job you hate, stay in a broken relationship or believe that all you have is the maximum you can ever achieve then the ray gun is pointed at nothing. When you follow your heart and trust your subconscious (or gut feeling if you prefer) the beam shines onto what you are passionate about. Rock stars become multimillionaire super star performers because they follow their passion and do what they love. Then they become bored with churning out the same material year after year but they are now trapped in a lifestyle. The fans want to hear the big songs they love and the concert promoters demand that the band give the paying audience what they want. Rock stars change from following their heart and creating what they love to nothing more than a glamorous and adored jukebox. They tour the world playing stadiums, going through the same list of songs, in the same order. Night after night, month after month and year after year. In the beginning nobody expected anything of him or her other than to do the thing they love. Fast forward past the peak of their success and now they have an agent, PR person, concert promoter, ex-wife, girlfriend and a drug dealer who all demand that the money flows at the same rate it always did. They simply can't stop working at the sausage factory or to even slow down, and so they lose their life purpose. The cavity appears and grows so big, so quick that it can't be filled and life becomes pointless and painful.

One magic ray gun per person! But with no training, no manual and no safety switch. This is the situation we have to deal with, you can choose to see it as a blessing or a curse – regardless the gun will just do what it does. Because we only have one of these guns, it can only be pointed at one thing at a time and so it is not possible to manifest more money if you are busy pointing the gun at the belief that money is scarce and difficult to come by. You can't become a good public speaker as long as the beam is currently pointed at being a poor performer in this area. If you want more confidence be tunnel visional about being in that state and always be aware when you have started thinking about the opposite position to what you want.

Obviously for me to tell you not to think about your crummy relationship with your husband is as effective a solution as telling you not to think about how you right foot feels. Until I said 'right foot' you were probably not even aware of it at all, then despite me telling you not to think about it you instantly became aware of it and are probably still aware of it right now. I accept that you will still worry about that failing relationship, that is natural and to be expected. However, what I want you to change is how long you allow the thought to remain. Become adept at spotting the negative thought, acknowledging it happened and then deliberately visualizing the opposite. Many successful sports stars use this technique to sharpen and enhance their game. Legendary golfer Jack Nicklaus famously said *"I never hit a shot, not even in practice, without having a very sharp, in-focus picture of it in my head. First I see the ball where I want it to finish, nice and white and sitting up high on the bright green grass. Then the scene quickly changes, and I see the ball going there: its path, trajectory, and shape, even its behavior on landing. Then there is a sort of fade-out, and the next scene shows me making the kind of swing that will turn the previous images into reality."*

In 1992, Anne Isaac conducted a study, which examined the influence of mental practice on sports skills. While most of the previous studies on this topic showed positive effects of mental rehearsal, they were not performed in actual field context using subjects who learned actual sport skills rather than just novel motor tasks. Isaac eliminated this problem in her experiment. She also tested the hypothesis of whether people who have better images and control over their images result in better performances. Isaac tested 78 subjects and classified them as novice or experienced trampolinists. Then she further divided the two groups into an experimental and control group. She also classified the subjects as either high or low imagers based on initial skill level. Both groups were trained in three skills over a six-week period. In order to prevent confounds, the imagery group was unknown to the experimenter until afterwards.

The experimental group physically practiced the skill for 2-1/2 minutes, which was then followed by 5 minutes of mental practice. Lastly, an additional 2-1/2 minutes of physical practice followed the mental practice. Meanwhile, the control group physically worked on the skill for 2-1/2 minutes, which was then followed by 5 minutes of a session trying a mental task of an abstract nature, such as math problems, puzzles, and deleting vowels. Then, 2-1/2 more minutes were spent physically working on the skill again.

The outcome of the experiment was as follows: there existed a significant difference in the improvement of the high and low imagers. In both novice and experimental groups where the initial skill ability was similar, the high imagery groups showed significantly more improvement than the low imagery group.

The reason visual imagery works, lies in the fact that when you imagine yourself performing to perfection and doing precisely what your heart desires, you are actually creating physical neural patterns in your brain, just as if you had really performed the action. These patterns are similar to small tracks engraved in the brain cells that can ultimately enable an athlete to perform physical feats by simply mentally practicing the move. Hence, mental imagery is intended to train our minds and create the neural patterns in our brain to teach our muscles to do exactly what we want them to do.

So before you try to communicate with that difficult person at work or talk about your feelings with your wife, visualize what the scene would look like if it all went perfectly. See yourself perfectly explaining the problems in a calm and happy way – see, hear and feel all the things you will experience when it goes exactly the way you hope. See and feel your partner responding exactly as you hope they would. Do it over and over again and each time making it brighter, louder, more colorful and more tangible than the last time.

You should trust me on this because I have not only experienced it myself many times over but I have witnessed breathtaking life transformations in my Manifesting Magic club members using just this technique alone.

For more information on my online Manifesting Magic coaching club visit www.CraigBeck.com

The Third Principle

As always the books in the Manifesting Magic series are designed to be short but powerful. I have resisted the traditional author's urge to pad out the book, preferring instead to give you concise and easily actionable advice that you can absorb and implement into your life. For the final section of Manifesting Magical Relationships I want to deal directly with a common concern or even complaint with what you have read so far.

Most people can grasp the concept that you get what you give, and if you want more love then you should give more love. Where this principle hits a sticking point is with people in situations where they are getting the opposite of what they are giving. For example you may be a very loyal individual with strict morals over infidelity but you repeatedly find yourself with a partner who cheats on you. Or even more extreme perhaps you keep ending up in relationships that turn abusive, whether that abuse is mental or physical. It would be quite understandable for you to object to certain aspects of this book based on your situation.

What I want you to understand is that even though you are not giving out the negative behavior you are on the receiving end of, you are still manifesting it into your life. Remember, what I said about the magic ray gun (but with no safety switch). Whatever you point that gun at will manifest and without any protective filters to prevent you getting perfectly horrible outcomes. The problem is that this magical manifestation device resides in a part of your being that you are prevented from accessing on a conscious level. This may at first feel unfair or frustrating but trust me, it is a very good thing that you can't get access to this weapon of mass destruction/bliss. Your subconscious is in direct control of the ray gun and it is firing it every second of every day, bringing things into your life that it believes you want to appear. You might wonder how this part of you cannot grasp that a lot of the things it is bringing you are causing you pain and misery. But the subconscious has no ability to judge or question the commands being sent to it. If for most of your life you have looked in the mirror and said to yourself 'boy you are fat' then you are creating the reality 'I am fat'. Your subconscious receives the command and acts on it without judgments. If you believe that all bosses are assholes and every boss you ever had treated you with no respect, guess what scenario your subconscious is going to think is the reality you want repeated?

Don't misunderstand this function of your subconscious and pass judgment on it. Without it you would be dead by now. It has successfully created programs to stop you touching the hot stove; it knows how to get you across a busy road, what to do when you fall into water and how you should behave on the edge of a tall building. You subconscious mind contains millions of programs it has developed over the years and they all run without asking your permission. Imagine if you were crossing the road and an out of control automobile was heading straight for you. In less than a second your subconscious has assessed the threat and loaded the exact survival program to get you out of harms way. Would you like it to run the program immediately or ask your permission first?

You must have noticed some recurring themes in your life. Events and situations that keep happening to you over and over again. Or perhaps you have witnessed self-destructive routines in the lives of your friends and family. I have a friend called Brian who for the past thirty years has run the same relationship program over and over. Brian is desperate to find someone to love; he has been since I first met him nearly three decades ago.

Here is Brian's relationship program, the one I have witnessed being run many hundreds of times over the last thirty years.

1. Brian meets a girl.
2. The girl likes Brian.
3. Brian falls in love almost instantly.
4. Girl gets scared at how quick he is moving.
5. Girl starts to withdraw to try and slow him down.
6. Brian senses her withdrawal and his desire increases.
7. Brian tries to fix the situation by doing the exact opposite of what she needs to feel reassured.
8. Girl ends the relationship.
9. Brian is devastated and can't believe that she wasn't 'the one'.
10. Go to the beginning and start again.

I can't tell you how many times I have witnessed this subroutine run from beginning to end. Every time I get a phone call from Brian that starts with the line 'Hey Craig, I have met the most amazing woman' my heart sinks a little. In that moment I know we are about to go on the ten step journey that will involve a lot of Groundhog Day style conversations and eventually end up with me comforting a distraught Brian over yet another painful break up. Of course one day he could meet the true woman of his dreams BUT this can never happen until he breaks the program running in his subconscious mind.

The biggest problem that Brian has is that he doesn't even know that the program exists. I have told him many times but he denies it is possible and every new relationship comes along with the claim 'I know I have said this before but I know that with [INSERT WOMAN'S NAME] it is going to be different'. The biggest problem that you have is that you are equally unaware of most of your own self-destructive routines. Worse than that, even if you were aware of them there is very little you can do consciously to remove them (because you are prevented from accessing the place they are stored). To demonstrate what I mean, imagine for me that I pick up my cell phone, call you right now and scream down the phone 'help I have locked myself out of my home' then my battery dies and the call disconnects. There is no way you can assist with this problem because you don't know where I live and even if you did you don't have a key to open the door anyway. I would be wasting my time asking you to help and you are wasting your time trying to arm wrestle the bad programs out of your head.

So how do you deal with problems that reside in a location you can't access? If you can't pin point the offending area of your subconscious you must clean the whole of it. This spiritual cleaning is the concept of embracing stillness and allowing the ego damaged areas of your being to be repaired by a force greater than you. There are many ways to achieve this from yoga and meditation to chanting and drumming exercises. However, the most powerfully effective solution I have ever found is something called Ho'opono'pono.

If you don't already know about the ancient Hawaiian healing method called Ho'oponopono, then please trust me on this… I am about to change your life!

Ho'oponopono is the ancient Hawaiian spiritual process of acceptance, forgiveness and gratitude. This is easily the most powerful knowledge I have learnt in my life to date. This amazingly simple and yet 100% effective process begins with accepting responsibility for everything in your life. When I say everything I mean EVERYTHING! If you want to improve your life beyond your wildest dreams you must completely forget about the concept of blame and throw away our predisposition of deciding certain situations are 'someone else's problem'. This profound wisdom starts with the lesson that your awareness of something makes it your responsibility. This does not mean it is your fault but fixing it is your job, whether it is something happening to you or just someone you know.

This concept is a little tricky to accept initially because your ego wants to fight against the accusations of blame. It also doesn't particularly care about the well being of other people and doesn't want you to waste precious effort enhancing anyone's life but your own. The ego is, as it always is... insane and when you learn to ignore it and take 100% responsibility for everything in your life, at that point magical things will start happening to you.

What does 100% responsibility mean?

It means that you accept that separation from others is an illusion and that if something is happening to someone else it must also be happening to you. You create everything you become aware of and only you can either give gratitude for that thing or clean it, if it is causing pain (for you or another). Everything you label good and bad about your life has been created by the divine power of your subconscious and soul. Essentially because you are a fragment of God you have the power of God, but unfortunately your ego interferes and causes big problems. It is a bit like giving a twelve year old the keys to a two hundred mile an hour Lamborghini and asking him not to crash it.

As the ego continually struggles to avoid fear and gain pleasure it inadvertently passes erroneous programs to the subconscious. As this part of you doesn't judge or question, it simply runs the program and before you know what is happening a whole heap of misery is being delivered into your life. It seems entirely illogical that you would create such pain for yourself and so you start looking for someone else to blame. This principle applies to everything in your life and the life of those around you.

- *If you are overweight and unhappy about the size and shape of your body then you must accept that you are responsible for creating this situation. You can no longer blame your genes, big bones, the proximity of the donut shop to your place of work or your parents.*

- *If your friend is having money trouble – this is your responsibility. I do not mean you have to bail her out or beat yourself up and feel equally as miserable as they do but you must accept that your awareness of it means it exists within you.*

- *Your boss is being a jerk and making your life miserable at work. His behaviour is your responsibility.*

I will say again… accepting 100% responsibility does not mean all these things are your fault. The concept of fault becomes irrelevant at the point we give up on the blame game. It might sound crazy, or just plain metaphorical, that the world is your creation. But if you look carefully, you will realize that whatever you call the world and perceive as the world is your world, it is the projection of your own mind.

If you go to a party you can see how in the same place, with the same light, the same people, the same food, drink, music and atmosphere, some will enjoy themselves while others will be bored, some will be overenthusiastic and some depressed, some will be talkative and others will be silent.

The "out there" for every one of them seems the same, but if one were to connect their brains to machines, immediately it would show how different areas of the brain would come alive, how different perceptions there are from one person to the next. So even if they apparently share it, the "out there" is not the same for them, let alone their inner world, their emotions.

Joe Vitale introduced me to this ancient wisdom through the book 'Zero Limits', which he co-wrote with a rather unusual clinical psychologist called Dr Hew Len.

More than thirty years ago, in Hawaii, at the Hawaii State Hospital, there was a special ward, a clinic for the mentally ill criminals. People who had committed extremely serious crimes were assigned there either because they had a very deep mental disorder or because they needed to be checked to see if they were sane enough to stand trial. They had committed murder, rape, kidnapping or other such crimes. According to a nurse that worked there in those years, the place was so bleak that not even the paint could stick to the walls; everything was decaying, terrifying, and repulsive. No day would pass without a patient-inmate attacking another inmate or a member of the staff.

The people working there were so frightened that they would walk close to the walls if they saw an inmate coming their way in a corridor, even though they were all shackled, all the time. The inmates would never be brought outside to get fresh air because of their relentlessly threatening attitude. The scarcity of staff was a chronic occurrence. Nurses, wardens, and employees would prefer to be on sick-leave most of the time in order not to confront such a depressive and dangerous environment.

One day, a newly appointed clinical psychologist, a Dr. Stanley Hew Len, arrived at the ward. The nurses rolled their eyes, bracing themselves for one more guy that was going to bug them with new theories and proposals to fix the horrid situation, who would walk away as soon as things became unpleasant, around a month later, usually. However, this new doctor wouldn't do anything like that. Actually, he didn't seem to be doing anything in particular, except just coming in and always being cheerful and smiling, in a very natural, relaxed way. He wasn't even particularly early in arriving every morning. From time to time he would ask for the files of the inmates.

He never tried to see them personally, though. Apparently he just sat in an office, looked at their files, and to members of the staff who showed an interest he would tell them about a weird thing called Ho'oponopono. Little by little things started to change in the hospital. One day somebody would try again to paint those walls and they actually stayed painted, making the environment more palatable. The gardens started being taken care of, some tennis courts were repaired and some prisoners that up until then would never be allowed to go outside started playing tennis with the staff. Other prisoners would be allowed out of their shackles, or would receive less heavy pharmacological drugs. More and more obtained permission to go outside, unshackled, without causing trouble to the hospital's employees.

In the end, the atmosphere changed so much that the staff was not on sick leave any more. Prisoners gradually started to be released. Dr. Hew Len worked there close to four years. In the end, there remained only a couple of inmates that were eventually relocated elsewhere, and the clinic for the mentally insane criminals had to close.

There are seminars where they teach you the many tricks to help you perform the process of ho 'oponopono, but according to Joe Vitale, Dr. Hew Len himself uses the simplest of the formulas. Whenever a matter arises –and they arise incessantly– addressing the Divine within you, you only have to say: I'm sorry, Please forgive me, Thank You, I Love you.

If you want to discover more about the origins and evidence of Ho'oponopono, look out for a book by Joe Vitale called Zero Limits. Joe goes into great detail about how this amazing principle, which has been passed down the ages literally creates miracles.

What you will discover if you download one of my subconscious reprogramming tracks is that there are distinct traces of this method running through every recording. Whilst you will rarely hear me make reference to Ho'oponopono, you will most certainly hear me use the words 'I am sorry, please forgive me, thank you and I love you' throughout the hypnosis tracks.

Whether you are just trying to stop smoking or are looking to attract the person of your dreams into your life you will find a subattraction ™ download that targets your precise desire or problem via the website at craigbeck.com

If you want to start manifesting the life of your dreams, you must simply accept your imperfection and seek forgiveness for it. I absolutely do not mean you need to apologize in the Catholic confessional sense of the word, heaping a gigantic load of shame on your own shoulders. This guilt achieves nothing, your acceptance and apology is simply a way of stating that you understand there is something manmade within you that is preventing divinity flowing. God/Source/The Universe is not disappointed, annoyed or ashamed of you, as all those emotions are purely human states and not relevant to a perfect source of creation. You cannot clear the bad programming or erroneous beliefs in your subconscious with your conscious mind, it simply isn't powerful enough.

Only the universe can clean the misaligned patterns and it's through this apology that you allow the process to begin. You are completely unaware of what beliefs are hidden and so you can't even begin to find them. Just accept that they are there, that they are your complete responsibility and you are sorry for their very existence. Ask the universe, source, divinity, God or whatever you want to call it, to forgive you and your bad programming. Ask for it to be erased and replaced with nothing, a void that can be filled with the pure white light of divinity.

As you begin this process you will start to feel that your life is like a vase full of water, when the container is empty of joy and love, you feel disconnected from source. When the vase is full to the brim the contents soon go stale like a stagnant pond. To achieve perfection in life the contents of the vase must continually be flowing. As you empty that vase of love into other people's lives it creates space for more love to flow in.

Create the space daily for more love to flow into your life by giving away as much as you can, there will always be an abundance if you have the space to receive what is waiting and willing to come into your life.

Let's recap the principles for Manifesting Magic relationships:

1. Accept that what you see isn't real. People rarely act the way they do to hurt you. We are all doing the best we can with the resources we have. We are all trying to run away from pain or towards pleasure.

2. Life is a big boomerang – be careful what you throw out there because it's going to come straight back at you.

3. You are 100% responsible for everything in your life. This life is your manifestation, it is your creation. If you are unhappy with elements of it (or specific relationships) you have the power to clean the broken programs and replace them with new 'life enhancing' ones.

All there is to do is clean!

Secret 4 - Thoughts Are Things

"Man's status in the natural world is determined, therefore, by the quality of his thinking", Manly P. Hall, The Secret Teachings of All Ages

What causes the man or woman to be "bowed down by age?" What causes the stooping shoulders, the weakened knees, the tottering gait? Because they believe only in the earthly and perishable. The spirit is not earthly nor perishable. But you can load it down literally with an earthy quality of thought which will "bow it down toward the earth with such burden."

It is not the physical body of the old person that is bent and bowed down. It is that part which is the force moving the body, that is, his or her spirit loaded with material thought which it cannot appropriate or assimilate, which becomes so bent, bowed and weak. The body is always an external correspondence of your mind or spirit.

A body thus ever renewing, beautifying, freshening and strengthening means a mind behind it ever renewing with new ideas, plans, hope, purpose and aspiration. Life eternal is not the half dead life of extreme old age.

The person who can see only the physical side and temporary expression of life, who eats and drinks in the belief that only the body is affected by less eating and drinking, who believes that the body is sustained only by force, generated within itself, and that it is not fed of an unseen element coming from the spiritual realm of element, and who believes that nothing exists but what he can see, hear and feel with the physical sense (that is the material which is always the temporary and perishable), draws to himself mostly those forces and elements which cause the temporary and perishable, and these acting in his body make it temporary and perishable.

Death of the body begins with thousands many years before they are in their coffins. The pale face, and parchment-colored skin, means a half dead skin. It means a portion of the body on which the spirit works the casting-out process of dead element, and taking on of the new very imperfectly. In the freshness of infancy and early youth, the spirit cast out and took on more vigorously. As years went on untruth was absorbed by that spirit. Its growth in knowledge was more and more retarded. Responding physical changes became slower and slower. The body commences to show "signs of age," that is to die. Because such spirit was less and less fed of that element which brings constant renewal of new thought which is new life.

So far does the belief and faith in weakness and decay prevail with the race that wisdom is often allegorically portrayed as an old man, gray, baldheaded, bowed and sustained by a staff. That means a wisdom which cannot prevent its own body from falling to pieces. In that form of being we call the child (a spirit or mind having come in possession of a new body), there is for a period a greater spiritual wisdom than when the child is physically more matured. It is the unconscious wisdom of intuition. It is for a time more open to the truth. For such reason, up to the age of eighteen or twenty, the spiritual casting off and taking on processes with the body are more perfectly performed. These relatively rapid changes in the physical maintain the bloom and freshness of youth. Sooner or later, however, the higher spiritual process ceases gradually to operate. Beliefs in the false, as taught or absorbed from others, materialize themselves in the body despite all the resistance of the higher mind as expressed in pain and sickness. The load of belief in the earthy and perishable accumulates. The body assumes an appearance in correspondence with such thought. At last the higher mind refuses longer to carry such a burden, flings it off, and leaves a dead body.

The death of the body is then the final process for casting off cruder element from the spirit, which it can no longer use or appropriate. But it is very desirable for the spirit to be able to keep a physical body which shall refine as the spirit refines, because in such equality of refinement between the spirit and its instrument, our increase in happiness is greatly advanced, and the relatively perfected rounding out of our powers cannot be realized until this union between spirit and body is effected.

Without health, money is pointless. Without health, the fast sports car or the gorgeous diamond ring on your finger are but purposeless trinkets. Yet if you ask most people what they need to be happy, all these material things are likely to be uttered before health and vitality get any consideration. We are similar to little magpies blinded by shiny things that catch the attention of our ego. Only when something dramatic happens in life do we become aware of how insignificant these bits of tin foil really are. If you have ever been seriously ill or witnessed someone you love in ill health then you will probably remember how irrelevant many parts of your life became. Areas that previously you may have described as 'your pride and joy'.

If I had started the Manifesting Magic series with this book then sales would probably have been so low that I would never have got around to writing part two. I started the series with money and financial wealth because it's an easy and broad carrot to dangle. Health is a bit like WIFI, we only notice it when it's not there or not as good as we want it to be. Think about that for a moment, if you have a reliable Internet connection in your home you probably don't wake up each morning grab hold of your phone to check Facebook and think 'wow the WIFI is working'. We ignore our good health the same as we do any other thing that has become a utility in our life.

There is understandable tendency to look at your reflection in the mirror and say 'yes that's me, there I am'. However, you are no more the reflection in the mirror than you are the car once you get inside it. The body you recklessly throw around this world is not who you are but rather a vehicle you are leasing. You have been lucky enough to inherit a multibillion-dollar piece of technology complete with the world's most powerful computer and an array of self-repairing parts. This machine is fully waterproof, adaptive and self-learning – truly a priceless and miraculous container for your life force. Of course very few people treat their body with the respect it most certainly deserves. We are more likely to appreciate the body of someone else than our own and that is entirely understandable. We are inside looking out and used to watching life unfold before us, rarely do we pause to be aware of where we are in this moment.

Twenty years ago I decided to learn how to scuba dive and I signed up with an instructor on the Greek island of Rhodes. On day two of my diving qualification course we were to dive down to the bottom of the ocean and complete several training exercises. These were to include the one I dreaded the most, mask clearing. This drill involved removing your mask and dropping it on the sand in front of you. You were then required to ignore the salty seawater burning your eyes and half blind find the mask before replacing it on your face and clearing the water by blowing air out your nose. All this is done twenty feet under water with a lead weight belt around your waist and a heavy scuba cylinder on your back.

I will be totally honest with you I did not want to do this part of the course and I could feel my flight or fight response kicking in as we sat on the boat waiting to get in the water. Now, basically my flight or fight response was suggesting two options. Either to fight George, the super-fit ex Greek military diving instructor or jump over board and swim a mile back to shore. As options go it wasn't a great situation to be in, so I decided that I would just have to suck it up and get it done. I told myself that I would try my best and insisted that I was not going to mess it up – what could go wrong?

I took a giant stride off the back of the boat and floated on the surface as I nervously waited for the rest of the students to jump in and for George to give us the thumbs down signal that it was time to deflate our jackets and descend into the deep blue. I gripped my regulator and sucked in to make sure it was functioning correctly. The cold pressurized air burst into my mouth and I took four or five deep breaths to be absolutely sure it was working. But something was wrong; I noticed after a few breaths that no matter how hard I sucked I wasn't quite getting enough air. I indicated to George that I had a problem and he swam over and checked the regulator for himself. He shrugged and said 'it's fine, okay lets go down'. I was in a blind panic, how could he not tell that I had a defective regulator and why was he continuing with the dive when I was going to struggle to breathe, something I very much enjoy doing.

I again insisted that the regulator was broken and with a frustrated expression on his face he tried it for himself. I was sure that now he would realize that I had been right all along and the dive would be aborted until all the equipment had been checked. George looked at me and said 'It's fine, now stop being a girl and dive'. Now wait a cotton picking minute, when did wanting to breathe become something only girls want to do. Yeah George,

God damn all those sissy boys who insist on breathing – the wimps!

Extremely unimpressed and exceptionally worried I deflated my jacket and dropped slowly to the bottom of the Ocean. The group of students learning to dive with me numbered six in total and we all kneeled on the sand in a semi-circle around George, who demonstrated the mask clearing exercise. One by one my fellow students completed the difficult task with ease and gave the OKAY symbol with their hands that they had cleared the mask and were happy. By the time it came to me I was almost passing out; I simply wasn't getting enough air. My chest felt like I had an elephant sitting on it and my head was spinning like I had just received a jaw-crunching blow from Mike Tyson. George seemed oblivious to the problems with my equipment and he pointed at me, indicating that I should remove my mask. All I could think was, Jeez George I am just about struggling to cling on to consciousness and you want me to add blindness into the mix for good measure!

I couldn't handle it anymore I indicated to George that something was wrong and I inflated my buoyancy control jacket to shot up to the surface, where upon I ripped the regulator from my mouth and breathed like a marathon runner crossing the finish line with after making a final sprint for the end. George surfaced a few seconds later and went crazy, shouting and chastising me for surfacing without permission and not doing the exercise.

My question for you dear reader is, who was right... the scuba expert or the novice student?

You can probably guess by the way I phrased the question that it wasn't me. The equipment was fine and so why could I not breathe? Anxiety is the answer! Anxiety creates shallow breathing patterns and shallow breathing patterns create anxiety. And so a loop or spiral is created, the more you breathe like this the more anxious you become. In this particular case I was sucking in big mouthfuls of air but only exhaling half the amount I had taken in, so eventually my lungs were full and yet I still had the urge to breathe. My assumption was that the regulator was broken, the reality was there was nowhere for the air to go. Once under the water, because I was not exhaling correctly my blood was filling with carbon dioxide and making me feel dizzy. Yet, all the evidence was pointing to the fact I had a defective piece of equipment – this was not even slightly true!

There are a few lessons to be learned from this incident not least that human beings are absolutely appalling at predicating the future. I assumed a lot of erroneous stuff and you know what they say about the word 'assume'… 'assume makes and ass of you and me', and it really does! I am sure you have your own stories of times when you were one hundred percent convinced that disaster was about to unfold and as it turned out, everything was okay in the end, or in the very least you could easily deal with the actual outcome that arrived. I felt very silly when I was safely back on the dive boat and I realized that there was nothing wrong with my equipment but I also know that in that moment on the bottom of the sea I was completely convinced that I was right and I was at serious risk of death. Logic did not exist at the time, I really should have been aware that George would not let one of his students dive with defective gear and with all his experience he would have easily been able to spot if there was a genuine emergency under the water. Logic should have told me that I was only twenty feet under the water, if my air had completely failed I could have easily swam up to the surface from that depth but nothing existed except my ego, terrified of the approach of death, screaming and screaming in my head to get the hell out of this situation.

Is this not exactly what it feels like when you walk up to the podium to make that presentation, stand to make a speech or start to walk towards the hot guy or girl you want to ask for a date? Alarm bells ring, sirens sound and your ego goes crazy, demanding to know what the hell you are doing something so dangerous for. As you persist in the task it does everything it can to get you to abort the mission. It forces your body to flood with adrenaline so you are ready to run or fight. Your heart rate increases so your muscles are full of speed giving oxygen and your breathing increases to replace all that oxygen that is now being ripped from your lungs and sent all over your body.

All this activity feels horrendous, just like it feels as a rollercoaster breaches the crests of the first incline and dangles for a brief second or two before the inevitable drop into oblivion. All these symptoms are the conscious mind predicting that disaster is about to occur and trying its best to move you away from danger. The intentions are good but the actions are inappropriate for the situation. So, you may be wondering how the conscious mind makes these predictions, I mean they must be based on some evidence otherwise you will feel like that at random times and not just when you were doing something significant. If this reaction of the mind is based on a whim you could be buttering bread or using the toilet when it suddenly happens – life would be unbearable. Yes, the conscious mind (or ego) is using evidence to predict the future but it is for the most part false evidence and out dated information. The good news is I can show you how to train the ego (like a naughty puppy) to stop responding to these predictions. In Manifesting Magic Part 5 we are going to talk in depth about fear (false evidence appearing real) and I will show you what creates it but more importantly what deletes it.

Right now, I want to meander back to the point of the chapter: one of my favorite hobbies… breathing. I absolutely love it and I try my very best to do it everyday. I joke, but breathing really is underrated, especially when it comes to happiness, peace & purpose. Eighty percent of the time we all live in a shallow, lazy breathing pattern. We sup the air around us and this means that only around half our lung capacity ever gets used. This is a shame because most of the oxygen absorbing material in our lungs is found in the lower most section. The very part of our lungs that rarely ever gets to experience exposure to the air, our breathing is far too shallow to get the air this far down into our body.

When you feel stressed, anxious or are desperately calling on your mind to give you the confidence you need your breathing rate increases but the depth and quality of each breath decreases. You become focused on getting air in quickly and forget that breathing is a two-part motion. Remember the yin and yang of life we talked about earlier… you must breathe in to be able to breathe out and vice versa. When you lose the balance of this motion and concentrate only on one aspect (breathing in) bad things start to happen. Our bodies operate at a surface gas ratio of seventy nine percent nitrogen and twenty one percent oxygen (this is different when we are underwater). If you do anything to mess with that ratio your body is going to object quite strongly.

When you fail to breathe properly the carbon dioxide in your body begins to increase. When carbon dioxide enters the brain it makes you feel sleepy and drunk in the early stages until eventually you pass out. It's pretty hard to act with any degree of integrity and self-belief when the gas mixture in your brain is intoxicating you. You wouldn't drink ten pints of beer before an important presentation at work (I hope) and so you should consider breathing poorly to be equally as ill advised an act.

It may seem unlikely that breathing correctly can have such a dramatic effect on your health and happiness but as always I challenge you to do this for 21 days before you pass judgment, you will be surprised at what happens. Everyday and as often as you can I want you to just stop what you are doing and pause life for a moment.

Breathe in slowly and deeply, hold your breath for a couple of seconds and then allow the air to slowly release from your mouth. Get your breathing into a nice regular rhythm and then observe the moment for all that it is. Notice things that you normally ignore or take for granted. Become aware of how your clothing feels against your skin, the colors in the sky and sunlight entering your eyes, the smell and temperature of the air around you. The objective here is not to pass judgment on anything, I don't want you to look at the clouds in the sky and predict a storm is on the way or even that it is a beautiful day. The idea is to be at peace with the moment, let it be what it wants to be without your interference or comment. If you can get into the habit of doing this a couple of times every day, you will be totally blown away by the dramatic affect that it has on your mental state and energy levels.

Please don't skip this exercise because later in the book it is going to become a fundamental part of a very magical process you are going to go through.

Tip: Hypnosis, mediation, yoga and many oriental martial arts focus heavily on breathing techniques. If you want to become a master of optimum breathing consider introducing one of these activities into your daily or weekly routine.

The Divine Power Inside

When my daughter was 5 years old she got a wart on her thumb. She hated this small but unsightly growth and would often come up to me with a very sad face and say 'Daddy I don't like this lump on my thumb, its nasty and I want it to go away'. One day I was walking past her bedroom door and I heard her crying inside. I walked in and found her sitting on her bed sobbing into her favorite teddy bear. I sat with her a while and discovered it was the usual problem that was causing her to be so upset. I told her that the wart didn't want her to feel like this and that if it knew how upset she was it would almost certainly decide to go. I instructed her to speak to the wart before she went to sleep at night and tell it to go. For a few evenings I would linger outside her bedroom door and hear her speaking very politely and kindly to this blemish on her thumb. She would say 'hello Mr. Wart, I hope you don't mind but I don't like you living on my thumb and I want you to go now'. It was very cute to hear and a perfect example of the beautiful innocence of children. They have a limitless imagination that has yet to be restrained by the rules of adulthood.

We all forgot about Aoife's wart until one day about a month later it suddenly popped into my mind and I asked my daughter to let me see it, I wanted to check if it had grown or changed shape. She looked at me like I was crazy and said in the most incredulous voice 'Daddy, don't you remember that I asked Mr. Wart to go away'. She showed me her hand and there was absolutely no sign of the offending wart. She wasn't at all surprised that it had vanished because I told her that it would, and she had no reason not to believe me. After all, I had also told her that Father Christmas comes with presents every year and that the tooth fairy never forgets to leave money in return for baby teeth. All those other magical things I had told her had come true so why wouldn't Mr. Wart disappear when asked politely.

Fast forward seven years and my now teenage little girl came up to me once again looking very sad. She told me she was getting bullied at school because she was getting acne on her face. She told me that in her desperation she had even tried asking the spots to go, but she explained to me that the magic doesn't work anymore and she added 'don't worry Dad I am not stupid I know it was never really was magic at all'.

The magic was very real and she was wrong to jump to that conclusion. One lesson I have learned the hard way with teenagers is you can't change their minds by telling them they are wrong. Hormones, boys and the gritty real world had got her; it was too late for Aoife and her magic! Of course magic exists and it is has even been proven time and time again by medical scientists all over the world. We very sensible and stern faced adults don't like the childish word 'magic' and so we call it something with a more grown up twang to it: 'The Placebo Effect', the label is of little importance but the results are the same. Essentially in the case of my daughter, the wart went because she entirely believed and expected it to do so.

Santa Claus comes on Christmas Eve, the Tooth Fairy buys teeth and warts leave when you ask them to.

Perhaps the spots stayed because she believed that the magic was just silly stuff from her childhood. The bible claims that Jesus performed countless miracles, not least the healing of the sick and crippled. Today with our uber cynical outlook on life many of us declare those fantastical tales to be nothing more than far fetched children's stories. However, the biggest problem with this debate is that the people who hold this view will see their opinion proved correct over and over again, giving them faith that they were right all along and anyone who believes otherwise is a fool. What they can't see is that they are being hoisted by their own petard, because we get what we believe whether that ends up being right or wrong. Essentially what I am saying is if you believe you have the divine power to heal yourself and manifest your own miracles then you will successfully prove that magic exists over and over again. However, if you believe all this stuff is for airy-fairy idiots with their head lost in the clouds then you will prove once and for all that magic is pure nonsense.

Is it really possible to use magic to heal ourselves? Faith Bryany wrote a wonderful book called Brain Sense and I want to share a little thought experiment that she suggests with you: Take three hundred harried commuters with headaches, not hard to do on the New York subway any workday rush hour. Of course, they are shouting and whining strident protests, which only worsen their headaches, which is precisely what you want. You reassure them that you'll get their names listed on the society pages of the *New York Times* in recognition of their public service (you can't afford to pay them), and that settles them down long enough for you to herd them into three soundproof rooms, one hundred headaches per room.

Now the fun begins. You do nothing with the first one hundred. They get to glare at one another Big-Apple-style and ruminate on their throbbing temples. You make an eloquent speech to the second group, informing them that they are the lucky recipients of a newly developed and powerful painkilling miracle drug. (It's actually aspirin with codeine, a proven pain reliever.) Then you leave them, too, alone with each other and their pain, contemplating their lawsuits against you. You make the same speech to the third one hundred, but you are lying to them. They think you are giving them a pain-relieving drug. In truth, they get a <u>sugar pill</u>.

After a half hour, you ask your three hundred captives to report on their headaches. In the "do nothing" group, twenty say their headaches are gone. Eighty are still suffering. In the second group, ninety report the complete disappearance of pain; that drug is certainly a miracle potion, the people say, and they wonder where they can purchase it. In the third group, the ones you deceived, forty-five still have headaches, but fifty-five do not. That pill did the trick, they say, happily re-boarding the subway pain-free. Your experiment was a success and you are off the hook, unless one of your subjects is a liability lawyer.

But forget the legal ramifications for now. Look at what the experiment revealed. A sugar pill has no physiological action that will cure a headache, but thirty-five of your headache-free subjects in the third group provide evidence to the contrary. (Why thirty-five and not fifty-five? Because the results from the "do nothing" group show headache pain will cease in 20 percent of your subjects after one-half hour regardless.) Thus, for 35 percent of the subjects in our thought experiment, the sugar pill was just as much a miracle drug as the painkiller the members of the "real drug" group received. This "cure" in the absence of any truly therapeutic agent is the placebo effect, and it's more than a curiosity. It's a direct result of brain action. But how?

Before we answer that question, we need to define precisely what the placebo effect is. It is not spontaneous remission. That's what the twenty people in the first group (and presumably twenty more in each of the other two groups as well) experienced. Some of us, no matter what the disease, get better for unknown reasons. The disease process simply reverses itself without any intervention. Whether remission is mere chance or the result of some self-healing process remains anybody's guess.

Neither is the placebo effect deception or self-delusion. The people whose headaches disappear after ingestion of the sugar pill are not lying, cheating, simple-minded, or insane. Their pain disappears--and not because they consciously wish it to. In study after study, where both subjects and experimenters are "blind" to the experimental conditions—that is, no one, including the researchers, knows who is getting the placebo—measurable, clinically replicable improvements in disease conditions occur in a sizeable fraction of all cases.

Furthermore, the placebo effect is no small or insignificant statistical aberration. Estimates of the placebo cure rate range from a low of 15 percent to a high of 72 percent. The longer the period of treatment and the larger the number of physician visits, the greater the placebo effect.

Finally, the placebo effect is not restricted to subjective self-reports of pain, mood, or attitude. Physical changes are real. For example, studies on asthma patients show less constriction of the bronchial tubes in patients for whom a placebo drug works.

The placebo effect is not deception, fluke, experimenter bias, or statistical anomaly. It is, instead, a product of expectation. The human brain anticipates outcomes, and anticipation produces those outcomes. The placebo effect is self-fulfilling prophecy, and it follows the patterns you'd predict if the brain were, indeed, producing its own desired outcomes. Researchers have found, for example:

- Placebos follow the same dose-response curve as real medicines. Two pills give more relief than one, and a larger capsule is better than a smaller one.
- Placebo injections do more than placebo pills.
- Substances that actually treat one condition but are used as a placebo for another have a greater placebo effect than sugar pills.
- The greater the pain, the greater the placebo effect. It's as if the more relief we desire, the more we attain.
- You don't have to be sick for a placebo to work. Placebo stimulants, placebo tranquilizers, even placebo alcohol produce predictable effects in healthy subjects.

As in all brain actions, the placebo effect is the product of chemical changes. Numerous studies have supported the conclusion that endorphins in the brain produce the placebo effect. In patients with chronic pain, for example, placebo responders were found to have higher concentrations of endorphins in their spinal fluid than placebo non-responders.

At one time, researchers viewed the placebo effect as an impediment--a statistical annoyance that got in the way of objectively evaluating the efficacy of potentially legitimate therapies. That view has changed. The placebo effect is today seen as an important part of the healing process. It's been studied as a treatment for Parkinson's disease, depression, chronic pain, and more. For large numbers of patients—the placebo responders—belief in the therapy will create or enhance its effectiveness.

In some respects, the placebo effect offers the best of all possible alternatives: therapeutic effects without the risk of negative side effects. That's why dozens of brain researchers are working to sort through the complexity of the numerous brain regions and neurotransmitters that produce placebo results. Theirs is no easy task. The placebo effect is not a single phenomenon, but the result of the complex interplay of anatomical, biochemical, and psychological factors. The same can be said for all our perceptions, I suspect. We see, hear, taste, touch, and smell pretty much what we expect to.

How powerful is this magic inside us? Headaches are one thing but what about serious illness such as cancer – does the magic work on the BIG C?

One of the more dramatic events regarding placebo therapy was reported in 1957 when a new wonder drug, Krebiozen, held promise as the final solution to the cancer problem. A patient with metastatic tumors and with fluid collection in his lungs, who demanded the daily intake of oxygen and the use of an oxygen mask, heard of Krebiozen. His doctor was participating in Krebiozen research and the patient begged him to be given the revolutionary drug.

Bent by the patient's hopelessness, the doctor did so and witnessed a miraculous recovery of the patient. His tumors melted and he returned to an almost normal lifestyle. The recovery didn't last long. The patient read articles about Krebiozen's not delivering what it promised in cancer therapy. The patient then had a relapse; his tumors were back. His doctor, deeply affected by the aggravation, resorted to a desperate trick. He told his patient that he had in his possession a new, improved version of Krebiozen. It was simply distilled water.

The patient fully recovered after the placebo treatment and remained functional for two months. The final verdict on Krebiozen, published in the press, proved the drug to be totally ineffective. That was the coup de grace for the patient, who died a few days later

But how deep can the placebo effect trespass into the well-defined area of medicine? Surely it can't joust with medicine's strike force; it cannot challenge surgery. Or can it?

In 1939, an Italian surgeon named Davide Fieschi invented a new technique for treating angina pectoris (chest pain due to ischaemia or lack of blood/oxygen getting to the heart muscle, usually due to obstruction of the coronary arteries). Reasoning that increased blood flow to the heart would reduce his patients' pain, he performed tiny incisions in their chests and tied knots on the two internal mammary arteries. Three quarters of the patients showed improvement; one quarter of them was cured. The surgical intervention became standard procedure for the treatment of angina for the next 20 years.

But in 1959, a young cardiologist, Leonard Cobb, put the Fieschi procedure to the test. He operated on 17 patients: on eight of them he followed the standard procedure; on the other nine he performed only the tiny incisions, letting the patients believe that they'd had the real thing. The result was a real upset: those who'd had the sham surgery did as well as those who'd had the Fieschi technique. That was the end of the Fieschi technique and the beginning of the documented surgical placebo effect.

In 1994, surgeon J. Bruce Moseley experimented with the surgical placebo. He split a small group of patients suffering from osteoarthritis of the knee into two equal groups. Both groups were told that they would undergo arthroscopic surgery, but only the first group got the real thing. The other group was left virtually untreated, with the doctor performing only tiny incisions to make the arthroscopic scenario credible. Similar results were reported in both groups.

Moseley, stunned by the outcome, decided to perform the trial with a larger statistical sample in order to reach safer conclusions. The results were replicated: arthroscopic surgery was equal therapeutically to the placebo effect.

I could fill a book ten times as large as this one with stories of placebo and magic but I am sure you get the idea and you are of course free to research and explore this phenomenon more if you wish. However, more evidence is only necessary if you do not believe and I suspect if you have reached volume four in the Manifesting Magic series then you are enlightened enough to already be open to the possibilities of divine magic. As always I want to keep these books free of any padding and fluff. I want you to be able to pick this book read it within a few hours and immediately apply the wisdom into your life.

If you have a recurring health concern or indeed any area of your life that is not serving you then keep it in mind. At the end of this book I am going to tell you the mantra that I have used to fix major problems in my own life, a mantra that has never ever failed. A mantra that has healed 100% of issues I have ever used it to address. However, first I need to explain how I discovered this secret and it was at a time when I needed it the most.

In book three I told you about the ancient healing process of Ho'oponopono. The very same principle that Dr. Hew Len used to cure a hospital ward full of mentally ill patients. In 2010 my world came crashing down around me, everything that could go wrong did exactly that. I was running a very large commercial radio station in the North East of England. I was earning more money than I ever had in my life and I was living a lifestyle that most would be envious of. Luxury homes, five star vacations, designer clothes and top end cars were all a part of my day to day life. Things were going wonderful with my job and just before Christmas 2009 I was offered a new contract in a new role with the company. This new contract had far less protection but much more remuneration. Essentially they were offering me fewer rights but more cash and greed won the day. The new money started to roll in and we had an amazing festive break. I returned to work in the New Year and found to my surprise that the company director (who was a big fan of mine) had been fired and replaced with a new guy. This new director immediately set about marking his territory and making key changes to the business. When he came across this very expensive guy with a very weak contract he saw the opportunity to send a dramatic message, and fired me with the only explanation of 'thanks for your service but we are going in a different direction now'.

I was a man in his mid thirties with two children and the outgoings of a football star. I had been fired for the first time in my life and the pain delivered to my ego was almost crippling. What I didn't know at the time was this was the beginning of the worst year of my life. I eventually found a new job but at fifty percent less than I was previously paid. The new position would require me to move two hundred miles away from my children and only see them at the weekends for a few hours and put enormous pressure on my relationship with my wife. I won't bore you with the full pity party of 2010 but by June I was on my knees. My health had crashed and I was constantly at the doctor's surgery, taking a colorful handful of different medications each morning. My financial situation had gone a similar route as Lehman brothers had and my marriage had collapsed beyond repair. I sat in my damp rented room with a pile of bills and divorce papers in one hand and a fist full of pills in the other. This was my lowest moment and I couldn't see a way out of the mess.

Let's skip the misery because it's getting boring, fast forward to December and everything has changed. My finances have turned around, I have stopped taking all the medication, I have lost 56lbs of fat and have a super toned fit and healthy body. My ex-wife and I have decided to keep the divorce as amicable as possible for the sake of the kids (we didn't even use lawyers – everything was agreed face to face) and I land a new job one hundred miles closer to my children. What caused such a dramatic turn around?

Magic…

I stopped blaming the world for my problems, I embraced the principles of Ho'oponopono and I accepted responsibility for all the issues in my life. I had to accept fully that losing my job had been my creation. The end of my marriage was my own manifestation and programs running in my subconscious mind had generated all the doom, gloom and poor health. I set about cleaning, and to do this I used a mantra called Morrnah's Prayer.

Morrnah was born in Honolulu, Hawaii on May 19, 1913 into the respected family of Kimokeo and Lilia Simeona. Her mother was one of the few remaining Kahuna Lapa'au kahea (one who uses words and chants to heal) and as such, became a lady-in-waiting to Queen Lili'uokalani, the last monarch and only woman to reign in the Kingdom of Hawaii, near the end of the monarch's life.

While there is no direct translation for "Kahuna," literally "Ka" means light and "huna" means secret, as in sacred wisdom. In English, "Kahuna" is often translated as shaman, priest, expert, or pejoratively, magician. However, a Kahuna, having the power of a shaman, the focused training of an expert, and the mystical links of a priest, is a spiritual leader and reverent caretaker of her or his community, merging the inner and outer worlds into blended harmony.

Morrnah was surrounded by this ancient oral healing tradition from the beginning. She grew up in a multidimensional world where inner and outer realities were fluid.

At age three, she was recognized to carry on this living tradition. Since the training was oral, handed down from teacher to student, there were not books to read, no notes to take. Morrnah learned by listening, repeating, and remembering. According to Martyn Kahekili Carruthers, "A student was expected to have a natural aptitude, a good memory, and to learn quickly. They were thoroughly tested. Instructions were given twice, with a maximum of three repetitions….Little time was wasted on the incompetent or slow."

In addition to her Kahuna training, Morrnah went to Catholic school where the way of Christ deeply influenced her spiritually. Eventually she went on to study the metaphysical traditions of India and China, and later the works of Edgar Cayce, the American psychic and past life researcher.

In the native Hawaiian community, a Kahuna served all equally and with respect. To a certain extent, the Kahuna was involved in every aspect of community life, healing mental, emotional, and physical illnesses as well as resolving broader disagreements. By mediating between the spiritual realms and the community, a Kahuna maintained a necessary balance of harmony. Healing took place in different ways, at different levels. According to Carruthers, "A Kahuna could often recognize and dissolve potential problems before they occurred. If a disease did not respond to la'au lapa'au (herbal remedies), lomilomi (massage) or la'au kahea (healing chants), then that disease was considered to represent an imbalance in the community. Ho'oponopono (family healing) might be required."

Morrnah lived the way of her ancestors as a valued member of her community, quietly practicing her gifts of healing for over half her life. She was a gentle soul who spoke little but felt a lot. She inspired relaxation, trust, and a sense of deep peace…she didn't try to explain things. One could just feel something special in her presence. My impression is that she was sending healing energy through her silence and intent. She was very loving and soft-spoken."

She said that "Western people have great difficulty in putting the intellect behind. It is difficult for the Western mind to get a grasp of a Higher Being because in traditional Western churches, the Higher Beings are not made evident."

She continued, "Western man has gone to the extremes with his intellectualism, it divides and keeps people separate. Man then becomes a destroyer because he manages and copes, rather than letting the perpetuating force of the Divinity flow through him for right action."

In 1976, when Morrnah was 63, she began to develop a new form of Ho'oponopono, modifying the original process.

Her system is simple and can be used successfully by anyone. The healing process includes one's soul and the Divine. Morrnah has said, "We can appeal to Divinity who knows our personal blueprint, for healing of all thoughts and memories that are holding us back at this time," she continued. "It is a matter of going beyond traditional means of accessing knowledge about ourselves.

"We are the sum total of our experiences, which is to say that we are burdened by our pasts. When we experience stress or fear in our lives, if we would look carefully, we would find that the cause is actually a memory. It is the emotions which are tied to these memories which affect us now. The subconscious associates an action or person in the present with something that happened in

the past. When this occurs, emotions are activated and stress is produced", Morrnah Nalamaku Simeona

The process of Ho'oponopono involves four phrases which can be repeated in any order:

1. I'm sorry
2. Please forgive me
3. Thank you
4. I love you

By saying these words over and over, a person is said to connect her/his own inner light with the light of Source. Over time, patterns in the subconscious dissolve, and by forgiving the parts within that hold those patterns, the person's outer world regains balance and harmony.

"Clean, erase, erase and find your own Shangri-La. Where? Within yourself. The process is essentially about freedom, complete freedom from the past," Morrnah said.

Morrnah was named a Living Treasure of Hawaii in 1983

In August, 1980 at the age of 67, Morrnah introduced this Ho'oponopono healing process at the Huna World Convention in Ponolu'u, Hawaii. She spent the next decade teaching Ho'oponopono throughout the United States, Asia and Europe. She also taught the Self Identity Ho'oponopono course at the University of Hawaii, Johns Hopkins University, and various medical facilities.

In the late fall of 1990, Morrnah embarked on her last tour of lectures and seminars, traveling throughout Europe and Jerusalem. In January, 1991 she returned to Germany where she lived quietly at a friend's home in Kirchheim, near Munich, until she passed away on February 11, 1992, at age 79.

Truly the biggest gift I can give you is to tell you the mantra that I used to fix my broken life. To use this miraculous healing process take yourself to a quiet peaceful place and spend a few moments doing the breathing exercise we talked about earlier. Allow all the stress and struggle of life to flow out of your body with each outward breath. Be present in the moment and slowly allow the issue you want to heal to come into your conscious thoughts. Try not to label or judge it and start to consider how grateful you would feel if it was removed from your life. Next slowly and rhythmically read Morrnah's prayer four times over. That is all it takes, you don't need to do it more than once but you can if it gives you peace.

This is my version of Morrnah's Prayer:

Dear universe, the Super-subconscious and all those who care about me in spirit. Please locate the origin of my feelings and thoughts of [INSERT ISSUE]

Take each and every level, layer, area and aspect of my being to this origin.

Analyze it and resolve it perfectly with God's truth.

Come through all generations of time and eternity.

Healing every incident and its appendages based on the origin.

Please do it according to God's will until I am at the present filled with light and truth.

God's peace and love, forgiveness of myself for my incorrect perceptions.

Forgiveness of every person, place, circumstance and event that has contributed to these feelings and thoughts.

I am sorry, please forgive me, thank you, I love you

Secret 5 - The Bad News

"Remembering that I'll be dead soon is the most important tool I've ever encountered to help me make the big choices in life.

Almost everything--all external expectations, all pride, all fear of embarrassment or failure - these things just fall away in the face of death, leaving only what is truly important.

Remembering that you are going to die is the best way I know to avoid the trap of thinking you have something to lose. You are already naked. There is no reason not to follow your heart.

No one wants to die. Even people who want to go to heaven don't want to die to get there. And yet, death is the destination we all share. No one has ever escaped it, and that is how it should be, because death is very likely the single best invention of life. It's life's change agent. It clears out the old to make way for the new", Steve Jobs

Back when I first started out in the media industry as a cocky seventeen-year-old boy, I remember once being interviewed by a local newspaper. I had just been appointed as the new breakfast presenter for Radio Wyvern, in Worcestershire – a town near the southern Welsh border with England. At the time I was the youngest morning show host in the country and the pressure was on me to mature fast but also to quickly demonstrate that I was worthy of the risk some poor misguided programme director had taken by putting such a total newbie in this enormous position of power. The newspaper article had been arranged as a favor for the boss and so it was only ever going to be a light hearted affair. I didn't need to be too careful what I said because the journalist had been asked to write something that was nothing much more than a complimentary commercial for my new breakfast show. The depth and weight of those questions would hardly tax me further than 'what's your favorite color'.

It quickly became apparent that I was going to be given twenty harmless if somewhat inane questions to pad out an article about me that they would probably bury somewhere on page thirty seven, just next to the classified ads for surgical support stockings and lost pets. I answered each question quickly and honestly. The journalist would listen to my reply, sigh and scribble something down my reply on his note pad. After four or five questions I realized that I was boring the guy to death. Hey I was seventeen years old, nobody had told me how to speak to the press or even how to answer trivia about myself.

I decided I was going to have to spice up my answers and try to be a little more of a personality, after all I was guessing that was all this poor journo was clinging to for ammunition to write what might be the most tedious piece of copy in his career. After a few more questions I felt like

I was doing a little better, the journalist had smiled once and raised his eyebrows a few times. This, I decided meant that I was either doing really well or really bad, I wouldn't know for sure until I saw the actual newspaper the next day or I got called to the boss' office for the hair dryer treatment.

Question twelve was 'what is your biggest fear', I looked him square in the eye and paused a moment. Then I raised one eyebrow, Roger Moore style and said 'fear, is my only fear – everything else is child's play'. This answer immediately made me want to vomit. So putrid and contrived was it that on the anniversary of this interview I swear the same gut wrenching, bile-inducing sensation came over me every year for many years that followed, as some sort of divine punishment for saying something so pretentious and appalling.

Here I am twenty-five years later sitting on a train to London and for some reason that memory is as fresh as it was the day I uttered such trite nonsense. Shockingly, I now believe it may have leapt from the grey, murky bog of my mind because I may actually have been right. Now hold on a minute, I know that premise does not defend against such wanton pomposity and I still most deservedly require a good slapping about the chops until I beg for forgiveness. However, 'fear' is what I have come to recognize as the single biggest element that prevents me (and all of us) reaching our true potential and really living the life of our dreams. It is not logic, responsibility or contentment that keeps us trapped in underachievement but rather it is fear that holds the key to our jail cell.

Human behavior appears to be complex and multilayered but in reality it comes down to two simple elements. All human motivation is essentially a binary process, meaning that we are moved to do something or avoid doing something by a switch in our head, either being in one position or the other. All decisions, actions and deeds are made as a result of us either avoiding fear or pursuing pleasure, and that is pretty much it. The reason for everything we do comes down to this simple premise.

We can spend hours debating this issue (as I have done many times before) but trust me on this one, even the apparently self sacrificing actions of a parent for their child are still motivated by the emotions of fear and pleasure.

In the case of self-esteem and confidence the fear that prevents us performing as we could is 99.9% misplaced. Of course sometimes the fear we feel most definitely has a place and I am not suggesting you ignore that little voice in your head that suggests you can't safely jump from one tall building to another. The fear you feel just before you do your first parachute jump is a process of the human mind operating exactly as it should. Making you feel afraid in these moments is a form of self-preservation. It is the brain's way of saying 'hey if you carry on doing what you are doing there is a very good chance you will die, and you will most likely take me along with you'!

But the fear that suggests to you that you are not attractive enough to talk to the hot girl is a misfire of this process. The gut twisting anxiety you experience as you step up to make a presentation to the whole office is this life saving feature of the human mind misunderstanding the situation and trying to force you to exit an environment it has incorrectly judged to be dangerous.

Confidence, or rather the lack of it is a simple throw back to our earlier times as hunter-gatherers. Or putting it another way, we are witnessing and experiencing the time lag of evolution trying to catch up with and adapt to what modern life involves. The life of a human being in the western world today has changed so dramatically over the last few hundred years that it is almost incomparable to what our forefathers had to endure. Today we get upset and feel like we have had a bad day if we get cut up on the way to work, can't find a parking space in the lot or spill our latte on our favorite t-shirt.

Compared to the life threatening events that happened on a daily basis to the generations that went before us, all these things are embarrassingly trivial. As relatively recently as the 1800's the average life expectancy of a human male living in the United Kingdom was 39 years. With disease, unsafe working conditions and vigilantly justice commonplace someone at my tender age of 40 would be considered to be an old man. Perhaps my children have been correct all along when they insist I am incapable of appreciating their musical taste because I am so decrepit.

Bearing in mind that evolution is a painfully slow process that takes hundreds of thousands of years to make even the smallest adaptations to the design of our species, you can perhaps see why it is struggling to keep up with our rapidly changing modern lifestyles. Apple might bring out a new model of its products every year but Mother Nature does not!

Back when we were at constant risk of being attacked by not only wild animals but also our fellow uncivilized man the human mind developed systems to try and keep us alive despite the inherent danger around us. Perhaps the most famous of these is what we have called the 'flight or fight' response.

When our fight or flight response is activated, sequences of nerve cell fire and potent chemicals like adrenaline, noradrenaline and cortisol are released into our bloodstream. If you want to see just how dramatic these chemicals are, get food poisoning and watch what happens. I can tell you from recent experience you're your body uses these neuro chemicals to make you dance like you are nothing more than a puppet on a string. When the body detects you have ingested something dangerous, like rotten food or too much alcohol it needs to force you to evacuate the offending material and it doesn't want to waste time debating this with you. Vast amounts of chemicals are released by your central nervous system that make you feel incredibly ill, almost to the point where you feel like you are going to die. The next thing you know you are holding onto the toilet bowl like your life depended on it, screaming projectile vomit into the water. As a reward for doing as you were told the body now releases mind bending amounts of dopamine, which has the effect of making you feel instantly better – almost high. I don't advise you experience food poisoning to verify this for yourself, just trust me.

My apologies, a rather unpleasant tangent sidetracked me there for a moment. Getting back to how the mind instigate the flight or fight response. These patterns of neuro reactions and chemical releases force our body to undergo a series of very dramatic changes. Our respiratory rate increases. Blood is shunted away from our digestive tract and directed into our muscles and limbs, which require extra energy and fuel for running, fighting or maybe even both.

- Our pupils dilate
- Our awareness intensifies
- Our sight sharpens
- Our impulses quicken
- Our perception of pain diminishes.
- Our immune system mobilizes.
- We become prepared physically and psychologically for fight or flight.
- We scan and search our environment, "looking for the enemy."

When our fight or flight system is activated, we tend to perceive everything in our environment as a possible threat to our survival. By its very nature, the fight or flight system bypasses our rational mind—where our more well thought out beliefs exist, and instead it moves us into "attack" mode. This state of alertness causes us to perceive almost everything in our world as a possible threat to our survival. As such, we tend to see everyone and everything as a possible enemy. Like airport security during a terrorist threat, we are on the look out for every possible danger. We may overreact to the slightest comment. Our fear is exaggerated. Our thinking is distorted. We see everything through the filter of possible danger. We narrow our focus to those things that can harm us. Fear becomes the lens through which we see the world.

Our fight or flight response is designed to protect us from the proverbial saber tooth tigers that once lurked in the woods and fields around us, threatening our physical survival. At times when our actual physical survival is threatened, there is no greater response to have on our side. When activated, the fight or flight response causes a surge of adrenaline and other stress hormones to pump through our body. This surge is the force responsible for mothers lifting cars off their trapped children and for firemen heroically running into blazing houses to save endangered victims. The surge of adrenaline imbues us with heroism and courage at times when we are called upon to protect and defend the lives and values we cherish.

While this protective routine still has a valid place in our lives it does not need to be activated quite as much as it is being doing and certainly not in situations that are not dangerous such as making a PowerPoint presentation at work!

But 'flight or fight' is an incorrect moniker for this instinctive response to stress. There is a missing F in that much quoted saying. Actually the more common reaction in situations deemed to be high risk is not to fight or flee but rather to freeze.

Fight, Flight or FREEZE

I am sure at times you have felt that 'rabbit in the headlights' sensation, where you know what is expected of you but somehow you just can't bring yourself to move. There are no mistakes in nature and obviously removing your conscious ability to move, is a feature designed by evolution. If a giant brown bear enters your immediate environment and your subconscious programming decides that the absolutely best chance you have to remain alive is to play dead then the last thing it wants is your pesky (and weak) conscious mind to have a say on the decision. So it locks you down and despite how much you want to move you find that it is virtually impossible.

When you freeze before making a speech or feel like your tongue has been paralyzed the very moment the beautiful woman starts to talk to you this is simply the mind misreading the situation as dangerous and firing off one of your self-preservation routines. Of course the big question is how do you stop it doing this?

The answer to this question and the beginning of a life full of abundance and success lies in the preceding pages. All I ask at this point is that you don't try to skip ahead and find the magic bullet. You will find no such thing, there is no one sentence that on it's own can build your confidence. Success, as with everything else in life is not about the final destination it is all about the journey to get there.

What I have discovered in life is that pretty much anything worth having is slightly just outside your comfort zone. Whether it's launching your own business, winning the league in your chosen sport, getting the career you have dreamed of all your life or ending up with the man or woman who makes you think you just won the lottery every moment you are with them. None of these things are inside your comfort zone, they all require you to stretch and grow before you can reach them. As most people know the walls of your comfort zone are made of a very strong material called fear. In order to smash through these barriers you have to stare fear straight in the eyes and charge ahead regardless.

Fear (false evidence appearing real) is just an illusion, and I don't just mean certain types of fear. You might quite reasonably argue that the anxiousness you feel when you stand on the top of a tall building is a very valuable sensation to experience in that moment. Of course, sometimes fear serves you in the short term but the biggest problem we have, as an intelligent species is we believe that we have something to lose. The quote from Steve Jobs that I started this chapter with is perhaps the most profound paragraph I have ever heard and for that reason you will find it quoted verbatim in many of my books. You are going to die, not one of us is getting out of this alive. One day everything you ever worried about will become irrelevant dust. You are already naked, you always have been and there is not a single reason why you should not be following your dreams and living a life full of happiness, peace and purpose!

When this ride is over nobody is going to mention the day you risked it all and unsuccessfully went after that big promotion at work, nobody will recall the day you threw caution to the wind and gambled with rejection by approaching that beautiful girl you saw in the street. All this stuff is only significant to your own ego.

Law of attraction books like 'The Secret' tell you that if you want to be rich then act like a rich person, think like a rich person and express gratitude for your wealth before it arrives. I am telling you this will never work, UNLESS you believe you deserve it.

When you consider what you want in life, ask yourself; does it lie beyond a wall of fear you are never going to cross? If so, then you will always use the divine power within you to hold your dreams just slightly out of reach. No matter how positive your thinking gets, no matter how many affirmations you make or how much gratitude you express, fear is going to prevent you manifesting magic into your life.

In this book you will make friends with fear. I will show you how I recognize fear not as a warning or obstacle but rather as an indicator of an opening window of opportunity. I now know that when I am afraid to do something, then this is the universe telling me clearly and specifically what I have to do next. Fear is a very strong sign to me that an opportunity to learn, develop and grow has arrived. What most people see as an obstacle I see as the most powerful gift anyone can get and I am going to give the same paradigm to you, starting today.

V is for Victim

"Let me tell you something you already know. The world ain't all sunshine and rainbows. It's a very mean and nasty place, and I don't care how tough you are, it will beat you to your knees and keep you there permanently if you let it. You, me, or nobody is gonna hit as hard as life.

But it ain't about how hard you hit. It's about how hard you can get hit and keep moving forward; how much you can take and keep moving forward. That's how winning is done! Now, if you know what you're worth, then go out and get what you're worth. But you gotta be willing to take the hits, and not pointing fingers saying you ain't where you wanna be because of him, or her, or anybody. Cowards do that and that ain't you. You're better than that!

I'm always gonna love you, no matter what. No matter what happens. You're my son and you're my blood. You're the best thing in my life. But until you start believing in yourself, you ain't gonna have a life", Rocky Balboa

I want to tell you about Katie, I am sure you know her already, perhaps not the same Katie but certainly 'a Katie'. Poor Katie drew a bad hand in life; she didn't do great at school because as she tells the story the teachers were idiots. She always dreamed of a cool apartment overlooking the sea, with a little dog called

Jack. Unfortunately because her boss is an asshole she has to rent a crumby flat in a rough part of town and due to the fact the Mr. Brown the landlord is a total douche and doesn't allow pets she is not allowed to get a dog.

Talk to Katie yourself and she will tell you how unfair life is and how she deserves so much more than such and such a person and yet they have everything she wants. She will tell you that nobody really understands her and all her friends are two-faced bitches who are out to cause as much trouble as possible.

Is it possible that Katie just got an unlucky break in life, is there any chance that she is correct in her assessment of life? Let's put it this way, there is more chance of Donald Trump denouncing racism and promoting love and peace for all men than Katie being accurate in her assessment of why she is not living the life she wants. Katie is a victim and these victims are everywhere – we can't move for them. These are the people that believe life owes them something and they often spend an entire lifetime furious that the neighbor got yet another new car or so and so got promoted at work when they are quite clearly incompetent.

Victims not only suck the energy out of their own lives but anyone who comes close enough to get caught up in their vortex of doom. They are mood hoovers and I am almost certain you can think of at least a few people who fit perfectly into this description. Let's first talk about how you deal with this trait in other people and then I want you to have a little honesty session about areas of your life where you have adopted the roll of victim, because its easier than facing the hard truth.

How do you help a victim? The short answer is you can't, because they don't want to be helped. They like being the victim; it gives them a convenient explanation as to why their life blows chunks. On their deathbed you could ask them 'why didn't you live the life you were truly capable of' and they will have enough plausible deniability to stubbornly point at something or someone and say 'because of that'. All the time they are pointing a finger of blame at everything and everyone around them they are blissfully unaware they have three fingers pointed right back at them. It is really frustrating to care about a victim because you can see the huge untapped potential in them but they cannot. When they look in the mirror all they see is someone who has been badly treated by life.

If they are a family member, or even perhaps your son or daughter you will desperately try to help them see the truth but in my experience all you will end up doing is expending vast amounts of energy to get precisely nowhere with them. The harsh reality is this; we are all divine creators of life. We each have a fragment of God embedded within us and we all have the power to perform our own miracles. If we take decisive action and flow with the universe instead of kicking violently to go back up stream we can manifest breathtakingly amazing lives for ourselves. Victims have this power too but they choose to ignore it.

How to spot a victim

Victims have reasons, lots of them and often they seem entirely logical and plausible explanations.

- I am ill because the doctor gave me the wrong medicine
- I am poor because my boss is a jerk
- I got fired because I am a woman
- I got made redundant because I am black
- They won't employ me because I am white
- I can't quit drinking because it's the only pleasure I have left.
- I am too stressed to stop smoking

The list goes on and on and all of it is 100% proof bullshit. There are four certainties in this life. You will be born, you will die and in between you will pay tax and life will repeatedly knock you down. As Rocky Balboa says 'Ain't nothing going to hit as hard as life'. Getting knocked down is not bad luck anymore than turning on the tap and getting water could be considered luck. Life is getting knocked down, the choice is getting back up again looking it in the eye and saying 'is that all you got, hit me again but this time put some effort in it you big girl's blouse'.

The reason you can't help the victims is when they get knocked down they love it. It gives them what they want, an excuse not to get back up again. They are like boxers who are too tired to keep fighting hoping for one decent punch so they can fall down with dignity and stay the hell down until the referee counts ten.

Exercise

Stop reading for ten minutes and think about the victims in your life. Ask yourself who they are, how long they have been there and most importantly how much time are you spending trying to make them feel better. Which by the way is like trying to push oil uphill. Once you are clear about who these people are I want you to make a conscious decision to spend less and less time in their company – until they are no longer a part of your life. That's right I am asking you to fire the mood hovers in your life, you can't help them, they are not helping you so it's time for them to leave.

There is a way to help but it is almost certainly not what you are doing at the moment. If dumping them out of your life is not possible or you are not comfortable doing that then reduce the amount of time you spend with them and use the cleaning method I describe in detail in Manifesting Magic part 4. To do this you have to accept responsibility for your share of the problem. The fact that this person's victim mentality is present in your manifestation of the universe means that it exists within you at a subconscious level. Use the healing meditation of Ho'oponopono to clean the program within you and you will both reap the benefits.

But wait… what if you are the victim?

Are you a victim? This is a pretty easy question to answer; think of something in your life that you are not happy with. For example lets say you need more money.

Now with that problem in mind explain to yourself why this is your current situation. If you find you have answers and excuses readily available (such as because my boss keeps overlooking me for promotion) then you are operating in a victim mindset around this area. If your response is more positive and places responsibility on your own shoulders then you are in an abundance mindset (for example – I took a pay cut to change direction in my career but I know if I give this new job 100% I am going to earn ten times the amount I would have in the old role).

Having an abundance mindset always starts with you taking 100% responsibility. Let me give you an example from my own life. In 2007 I bought a villa in Cyprus, I didn't know it at the time but I was investing at possibly the worst time in the last century. Property prices were hugely overinflated and there was a mad rush of eager buyers trying to get in on what was being touted as a gold rush. Realtors were promising anyone who would listen that you could easily double your money within a few short years. I had always wanted to live in the sunshine by the sea so I went all in. Three months after I collected the keys to my property the Lehman Brothers collapsed and the whole western world went into a financial meltdown. Overnight my property lost 40% of its value but that was irrelevant, as the whole market had evaporated. Due to a concrete explosion over the past few years the tiny island of Cyprus found itself with thousands and thousands of new build property and absolutely no buyers to be seen. To make matters worse I had taken a mortgage in Swiss francs on the advice of the bank. Because Switzerland was considered a safe haven outside the crashing dollar, pound and euro their currency value went through the roof. My mortgage payments tripled over night.

Whose fault is this disastrous investment? The victim would say it's the realtor for advising me badly; it's the bank for selling me a volatile product or any other number of villains that could be pointed at and labeled as the 'fault' behind this mess. At the point where you create an excuse you become a reaction to life. You are a passenger who is responding to the events of life that are thrust upon you. Conversely when you accept 100% responsibility for the events around you then you are in the driving seat. Let me tell you, when you are alone in a runaway car the last place you want to be is in the passenger seat.

My thoughts about the house in Cyprus are this: It is my responsibility, I created it and I will solve it. I don't believe it was a mistake, I believe it is a blessing here in my life to push me in a specific direction, to challenge me, to teach me and ultimately to make me stronger. When the time is right the situation will resolve one way or another.

Exercise

Stop reading and grab a pen. I want you to write down everything negative in your life that you believe is there because someone else put it there. Then next to each bullet point I want you to come up with a new positive spin that gives you 100% responsibility for the event. Now wait, lets be clear. There is a huge difference between blame and responsibility. I am not asking you to take the blame for the day you got mugged in broad daylight or the night your car got stolen. Fault and blame are pointless actions of the ego, blaming the mugger for attacking you doesn't undo the act of violence that occurred.

What I want you to do here is accept the situation as being a part of your life. You may not have chosen to have it happen but for whatever reason you attracted it in. It's a part of you and that means you are the only person who can heal it within yourself. Make peace with it and try to give yourself a point of view that does precisely zero finger pointing and has a high expectation that a positive outcome will arrive.

These exercises are very easily skipped and forgotten about but please try to do them because they make a huge difference to the speed at which you can effect positive change in your life.

Forgive Yourself First

"As I walked out the door toward the gate that would lead to my freedom, I knew if I didn't leave my bitterness and hatred behind, I'd still be in prison", Nelson Mandela

It's almost a certainty that many years ago you buried some demons alive. The bad news is these beasts don't die they just change shape and eventually escape the grave. If you are holding onto any resentment, especially from your childhood, now is the time to let it go. Sometimes these issues are obvious, if you had an abusive childhood then you probably have a very specific person in mind already. However, sometimes they are a little subtler, despite this they are still capable of causing significant disruption to your inner state of peace. I am a good example of this latter situation.

Many years ago I recognized that I had two very profound issues. I had a very strong fear of rejection and also a fear of being constrained (not physically constrained but mentally). It's always much easier to deal with a problem that you know you have than to stumble around in the dark looking for the cause of your pain. However, what perplexed me with these specific problems was I had no idea where they had come from. My childhood was as close to perfect as you could get. I was lucky enough to grow up with both sets of parents; I was loved and wanted for nothing. I simply couldn't understand why I was such a 'fuck up' in various areas of my life.

One day I was in a spiritual bookstore in New York and I got talking to a woman who was also browsing the books on meditation. She was called Anne and she had such a peaceful aura about her and we ended up talking for about an hour, just standing there in this little store. We started to get quite deep about our lives and I told her this long-standing conundrum of mine. She listened carefully and asked a few pertinent questions. Specifically, she wanted to know if my mother had been very strict or overbearing. I told her that was not the case but my dad used to infuriate me. He was a real no nonsense sort of guy and he always seemed to spoil my adventures by telling me the outcome of everything I wanted to do before I had had a chance to try them. I would get excited by a new project, sport or activity and he would spoil it by telling me that I will get bored of it within a week and it will all have been a waste of my time. The only thing I hated more than him doing that was the fact that he was virtually always correct.

When I turned thirteen I couldn't take it any more and I asked if my parents would pay for me to live at school (my school had a small boarding contingency as many children had parents who were serving in the armed forces). I wanted to be around people my own age and out from under the scrutiny of my father. I needed the freedom to make my own mistakes and learn my own lessons. I told my parents what I wanted to do.

At this point in the story Anne became very interested, 'what did they say' she enquired and I told her that they were fine about it and simply said 'If that's what you want son'. To me this was no big deal but to my surprise Anne thought this was terrible, 'What you mean they didn't even try to stop you' she asked with a very concerned expression. I told her again that no they just said I could do anything I wanted. This she said was surely what was the cause of my fear of rejection; that my parents didn't fight to keep me close. It had been no hardship for them to be free of me at such a young age. I had never thought about it like that before. I don't know if that is the only cause of my issue but since this revelation and my acceptance of it I have felt significantly more peaceful in almost every situation.

It doesn't matter whether you have hulking great painful events or just a collection of minor scars, all must be forgiven before you can move on. This subject is a whole book in itself and I can't really do it justice in one chapter. However, I encourage you to address this challenge as soon as possible. There are several things you can do that may help:

1. One of the most effective ways to address buried feelings about events and people from your past is a technique called Timeline Therapy. This is a talking therapy where you mentally revisit past traumatic events under the guidance of a trained counselor. Rather than experience all the painful emotions again first hand you are encouraged to view the event as a third person, watching the situation unfold as though you are floating above it. This way you can detach yourself from the all encompassing feelings you experienced at the

time and try to see what was motivating the other person to treat you in such a way. It is good to remember that very few people are inherently evil, most negative behavior comes from fear in the other person. Bullies for example are not super strong, tough individuals but rather the opposite! Bullies are deeply afraid of something unspoken and use violence and intimidation to try to suppress that distress.

2. Timeline Therapy would be my preference but there is no doubt that any good, trained councilor will be able to help you release resentment and find peace with the traumatic events of your past. Perhaps you already know what your major fears and phobias are, if so then you have already taken the first step towards a solution. So why not decide right now that you are going to take action and deal with this once and for all. Unless of course your major demon is procrastination, then probably just do it tomorrow hey?

3. Perhaps the easiest and most cost effective solution can be found in the online members area of my VIP Club. Once you get started you will get access to my Demon Slayer Hypnosis downloads. You will find a complete range of subliminal reprogramming tracks designed to deal with everything from fear of rejection to body confidence and social anxiety issues.

The Illusion Of Permanency

Have you ever wondered how hugely successful Hollywood stars who appear to have everything in life anyone could possibly end up committing suicide? Despite the outside appearances these people believe they are trapped in a situation that can't ever get better, in short their misery appears to be permanent.

Permanency does not exist in any form in our world. Everything living, everything nature placed here and everything we build will eventually crumble and fall. Nothing is saved; death and destruction are like the outward breath of God. He breathes in and life is created, trees grown and buildings emerge. He breathes out and people die, trees burn to the ground and buildings collapse.

Sadam Hussain spent a lifetime building as many statues in his image as possible, he commissioned hundreds of portraits to be painted and even officially named Iraq's main airport Sadam Hussain International Airport. He did all this in a vain attempt to live on after his death – he failed. Virtually all the statues were pulled down and the airport was renamed.

If you are pinning your happiness and success in life on achieving permanency then you are destined to fail. At the end of your days when you lay in your deathbed considering your vast property portfolio and the millions of dollars in the bank you can be sure that you would happily trade it all for just one more week alive.

More subtly than that we all also get attached to the idea of permanency when we give ourselves labels. Do you not think at some point when Adolf Hitler was growing up his mother sat him on her knee and said 'Adolf you are such a good little boy'. Was she wrong, or perhaps she was right but only in that moment?

All too often we take these labels and decide that they are a permanent description of who we are.

- I am a good person (how do you know you always will be?)
- I am a fast sprinter (will that always be the case)
- I have high standards; I will never stay in a hotel with less than a 5 star rating (Never?)

When I coach people one to one they normally approach me with a label that they have decided is permanent. They come up to me and say 'I am a terrible public speaker, I always make a fool of myself' or 'I have terrible bad luck, nothing ever goes right for me'.

If you believe there is anything about your life that is permanent then I want you to spend some time thinking about how that could possibly be true in a world where it's impossible. I apply this just as much to the good stuff as the things we call 'bad'. I would call myself a 'good parent'; I love my children deeply and without question. However, I am willing to admit that at times I have made mistakes, given bad advice, shouted when I should have hugged and generally been a 'bad' parent. Especially during the challenging teenage years where my kids were striving to break free and be individuals. So which am I? 'A bad parent' or 'a good parent'? In reality no label serves any useful purpose beyond the moment it is expressed in.

Good times will end and life will blindside you with events that spoil the fun. In the dark times the storm will come to an end and bright sunshine will once again fill your life. This is the ebb and flow of the universe – God will breathe in and God will breathe out.

Fear, Your New BFF

"Fear keeps us focused on the past or worried about the future. If we can acknowledge our fear, we can realize that right now we are okay. Right now, today, we are still alive, and our bodies are working marvelously. Our eyes can still see the beautiful sky. Our ears can still hear the voices of our loved ones", Thich Nhat Hanh

A beautiful woman walks into a bar full of guys. Each man notices her, admires her and imagines himself with her. The married guys allow a little sigh to escape their lips and a few even curse the missed opportunity. But what about all the single guys, surely here is a perfect chance to at least talk to a stunningly attractive woman. A small but perfectly formed window of opportunity to find out if her personality lives up to her beauty. In 99.9% of occasions that woman will come and go without a single interaction – dozens of single guys deliberately opt out of the possibility of being her man on a daily basis… but why?

The answer is fear, while their heart says 'speak to her' the head (or rather their ego) says:

- She is too hot for me.
- She probably has a boyfriend.
- She looks busy, I would be annoying her.
- I bet she gets hit on all the time and is sick of it.
- She will laugh in my face

The excuses and reasons are endless and all of them are baseless or if you prefer, false evidence appearing real. None of those excuses are a valid reason not to speak to this amazing girl. They are all just pieces of graffiti that are sprayed on the walls of your comfort zone. As we approach the edge of the zone we notice that there are lots of brightly colored and aggressive looking warning signs. They scream that there is danger and risk beyond this point and for your own safety you should go no further!

Let's break down a couple of those excuses a little further:

She is too hot for me: Says who? Attraction is not a choice, we can't consciously make a decision to be attracted to someone or not – it just happens. I have been in relationships with women who have been up to 15 years younger than me, this does not mean all younger women are attracted to me – I wish, but sadly this is not the case. Attraction is not a choice, I have been rejected more times than I can remember but I don't take this personally and I am certainly not offended by it. Failure is never in the rejection but rather in deciding to take no action at all.

I have met truly awe-inspiring men and women over the years whom describe themselves as 'not that attractive'. I want to grab hold of them by their shirt collars and shake them until they see what I see. Only last month in London I was coaching a financial executive who looked after billions of pounds worth of stock options on a daily basis.

He was a partner in his firm and I quite quickly gathered that he is a total genius at what he does. As we sat in a coffee shop off Knightsbridge he relived the story of how he made his way from a council estate in Glasgow to living in a penthouse apartment in London worth over five million pounds. I was totally blown away by this guy and his story, then as he came to the end of the tale he looked me straight in the eye and said in his no nonsense Scottish accent 'shame I am such an ugly bastard right?', and laughed.

This guy considered himself to be unattractive and had spent most of the past decade single or in poor quality relationships that didn't serve him. In reality he is extremely intelligent, witty, charming and sophisticated man who has moved mountains to create pure success and abundance. I told him that there are millions of women on this planet who if they found a guy like him would think all their Christmases' had come at once.

We are all our own worst critic and yet most of us ask ourselves such important questions as 'am I attractive', "am I a good person" and 'what do I deserve in life'. We should not be surprised when we get a similar answer to when you ask the grumpy old men from the Muppets what they thought of the show!

She probably has a boyfriend: Yes this is a possibility but are you really saying that married people and those in long term relationships no longer enjoy feeling attractive to other people?

I don't know about you but I have found that it is often the married and long-term relationship gang who get the least compliments in life. If I see someone I find attractive I always make a point of going out of my way to tell them that. Quite often they will be shocked and blurt out 'oh I am married, sorry'. I will just say I know, smile and walk away. My intention was not to do anything other than make that person's day brighter.

If you are not speaking to people you are attracted to because you are afraid they are in a relationship and you will get rejected for that reason then you have this whole thing the wrong away around. You are not pushing through your comfort zone to get something, such as a phone number, a date or even sex but rather to give something of yourself away. You have the power to make everyone you meet (male and female) feel amazing, unique and special – not using this power is a crime.

Now, sometimes people are so used to living in a loveless world that they refuse to accept this gift from you. It happened to me yesterday, I was in the bank and the most stylish woman I have ever seen in my life walked in. She must have spent over four hours getting ready that day – she looked amazing. As is my custom I walked over to her and said 'Excuse me, just wanted to let you know that you look amazing'. I smiled and expected at least something comparable to a smile in return - I didn't get it. She curled up her lip and stared me straight in the eye and said 'go away'.

There is no point taking offense because I don't have enough data to understand why she reacted like that. Perhaps she was just dumped by her boyfriend, maybe she lost her job that morning or maybe she was just in one hell of a bad mood and everyone was getting that response that day. Who knows but what I do know is that the problem does not belong to me.

Yes, it is true that if you always obey the danger signs nailed to the outer walls of your comfort zone you will be protected from awkward situations like the one I just described. But you will also never experience the flip side of that scenario. I have amazing friends all over the world because I make strangers feel amazing on purpose. I consider the world to be my playground, I believe I can travel alone anywhere on the planet and leave having had an amazing time with a whole new group of friends. My current partner Ina is from Berlin, Germany. We met when I was there in January and saw her amazing smile behind the counter of a local deli. We got chatting and met up after she finished work – the rest they say is history. Fear did not want me to meet Ina, fear wanted me to keep walking and stay away from any chance of rejection – but that is not what I wanted.

I don't want this to become a book about pick up or solely about relationships. I want this to be a tool to release you from the life limiting loops created by fear. When we use the word fear we normally apply it to situations where we wrongly or rightly predict that we are at risk of harm. For example standing on the edge of a tall building generates a sensation of fear and anxiety so we become acutely aware of what could happen if we act inappropriately in those situations. We can be afraid before a job interview because we have become attached to an outcome and don't want to experience rejection followed by the loss of that outcome. However, fear isn't always this obvious or dramatic but it can still be hugely limiting in our life.

When people go on a diet they start out with good intentions and a desperate desire to improve the way they look and feel. An honorable pursuit, but why do nearly 95% of them not only end up putting back on all the weight they lost plus and additional few pounds for good measure? The answer is fear, at the start of the diet the pain of looking in the mirror or not being able to squeeze into their favorite denim any more creates low level fear. For example 'what if I just keep getting bigger', 'what if I have nothing to wear at the party', 'what if they start calling me names at school' etc. So, we start the diet motivated to move our chubby body away from the fear. Then we lose a bit of weight and the original fear subsides but it is often replaced by a new concern. You see, we enjoy our tasty treats and takeaways in front of a good movie. Suddenly we feel like we are depriving ourselves of some of the fun bits of life. We fear that if we carry on being strict with ourselves we are going to be short changed by life and have less fun. Thus begins the yo-yo diet routine that dominates the life of so many.

I am writing this section of the book in the business class cabin of a British Airways flight from London Heathrow to Austin, Texas and even here fear is present. I am not talking about worrying about the plane crashing or running into some scary turbulence. I have been on board for just two hours and so far I have been offered free alcohol at least half a dozen times. I can't drink alcohol because it has a nasty habit of trying to kill me. If you have read my book *Alcohol Lied to Me* you will know that I had a near two decade long battle with the booze and I became teetotal about six or seven years ago. I don't have to struggle to stay away from drinking, no part of me wants to go back where I was but there is an element of fear at the back of my head every time the airhostess comes down the aisle with the drinks trolley and I turn down a very expensive French Bordeaux and instead ask for a cheap glass of water. The northerner in me feels like I am getting ripped off – I feel like I am getting much poorer value for money than the guy next to me who has so far knocked back $100 worth of wine and brandy. I am 99% certain that I won't buckle in the name of value but I am acutely aware and afraid of that 1% that still lingers at the back of my mind.

Fear is present on a daily basis and in a myriad of ways. We are taught to be careful, to listen to fear and respond accordingly and the vast majority of society obeys this unwritten law. The result is a safer, more boring & less fulfilling life. This is the world of the Average Joe and the Average Jane – safe and steady but beige. What I am encouraging you to do is respond to fear in a highly counter intuitive way. Instead of seeing fear as a warning I want you to see it as an opportunity light blinking on the dashboard of your life. Essentially, if you are afraid of it then you must do it!

Fear Response Examples

Situation	Average Joe Response	Fearless Response
Afraid of drinking alcohol.	Path of least resistance. Surely just one won't hurt will it?	Take the least easy path. See it as a clear sign that drinking won't serve you.
Afraid to approach the hot girl.	Don't do anything – let her walk out of his life.	Approach without a second thought. See the fear as a green light.
Afraid to go through with the charity parachute jump.	Cancel for 'health reasons' explains to friends they would love to but the doctor said no.	Fear means there is no other option but to do the jump. Everything else will make their comfort zone contract.

I can't begin to tell you how many people I meet who are full of regret, and virtually never about the things they have done in their life but much more commonly about the things they never did. The last time I saw my aunty Angela she was having a coffee with my parents at their home in Darlington. I joined them all for a short while and as I sat down Angela was expressing her regret that she had never learned to drive. She had started to learn but got too afraid to ever put in for the test and it just became one of those things we label shoulda, woulda, coulda. Two years previously Angela had sadly been diagnosed with C.U.P. cancer (cancer of unknown primary origin). She was still her old lively self but her prognosis was not great, all treatment had ultimately failed. The doctors estimated she had between six and nine months to live. Angela decided that before it became impossible she was going to take and pass her driving test.

She never got the chance as she died three weeks later. The moment she died passing or failing that driving test became irrelevant; all the fear about taking the test in the first place also became equally as irrelevant. There are dozens of things that you want in life that you don't have because fear is preventing you going after them. One day in the future all that fear will be rendered pointless by the same event that Angela went through, the event that nobody has ever managed to avoid. What I am saying is that your ego is trying to protect you from harm by encouraging you to avoid risk by using fear as a virtual 10x4 to hit you about the head with.

Your body is like an apartment shared between two tenants. The ego and the soul, or if you prefer the conscious mind and the unconscious mind are the tenants of your body. The soul is eternal and divine, it is essentially a fragment of God and it knows this for certain. It is also acutely aware that the apartment it is renting is temporary and when the lease ends it will just move to a new place and start over. However, the ego knows that when the lease ends that's the end of the story, its game over. This creates a sensation of blind panic for the ego, which point blank refuses to accept the situation. It kicks and screams trying to prove that it can prevent the lease from ending. Hey perhaps if you fill the apartment with more and more stuff and never leave so they can't come in and dump your possessions then perhaps the lease will continue evermore right? The ego is so terrified of the end it has been rendered insane by the constant thought of it.

Out of this insanity we get all the self-limiting beliefs that hold us back.

- Save for a rainy day
- What can go wrong, will go wrong
- She's too hot for you, she will reject you
- You are not ready for your driving test
- You are not good enough for that promotion at work

The ego uses the past as a reverse projector in an attempt to control the uncontrollable. Fear is liberally applied to all areas of your life in the hope that it will keep you safe if completely unfulfilled. You are alive but miserable, that's good enough. The ego doesn't particularly care how happy you are, its primary focus is trying in vain to avoid the inevitable final act, at whatever cost.

What I am about to ask you to do is acknowledge that one of your tenants is insane and while you can't evict you can decide to stop listening to his/her insane ramblings. From this point on fear should be seen as the screams in the night of your troublesome tenant. All the predictions of doom, gloom, terror and trauma are nothing more than a desperate illusion.

Start living in the knowledge that the only moment that exists is this one, right here and right now. The past and the future do not exist and they never will – this is it and this is all there will ever be.

There is a percentage chance that this nineteen year old Boeing 777-200 aircraft will crash before I reach Austin, Texas – should I just stop writing now just in case? No of course not, because right here in this moment I am alive and as long as that situation continues I have a message to get out there.

Exercise:

I want you to stop reading at this point and take a little life inventory. Grab a pen and paper and write down everything you can think of that you have wanted to achieve but have been prevented doing so by fear. Perhaps you have always wanted to skydive but can't quite bring yourself to sign up for a jump. Maybe there is a senior position opening at work and you have told yourself that you are not quite ready and maybe try again in a few years. Perhaps you have been head over heals in love with Nicola on reception for years and never done anything about it?

On a blank piece of paper draw four columns, in the first column write your goal, in the second write down how fear is preventing you from achieving this goal, in the third column write down what will happen if you continue to let fear dominate this area of your life and in the final column I want you to imagine how you would feel if you ignored the 'Danger Do Not Pass' signs hanging on the wall of your comfort zone and charged on through regardless.

Example:

Goal	Fear	Failure	Success
To skydive	I might die, or worse I might embarrass myself by refusing to jump!	It will always be there as something that says 'you are a coward'.	I will feel invincible. I will have done something most people would never be brave enough to do. I would feel huge pride in myself.

One of the most positive motivational speakers that America ever produced was Zig Ziglar. He would describe the start of his day in such a beautiful way. He used to say 'every morning at 6am my opportunity clock would go off and wake me up. I don't call it an alarm clock because that's negative. That bell signals the start of a whole new day full of wonderful opportunities'.

As ever I want this to be a practical investment of your time and money, something that you can take and implement quickly into your life and consequently see massive positive change as a result. I am going to close this final chapter on fear with a challenge, for you to do one thing right now that fear has been making you avoid. It could be something as simple as picking up the phone and apologizing to someone you didn't act in the right way with. It could be clicking send on a resignation email or a job application form – find something that you are afraid of and embrace it as an opportunity.

I sincerely hope that this aircraft lands safely on the tarmac in Austin, Texas and this book gets to make it into your library of success and personal development downloads. If you are reading these words you are already in the top 20% of individuals of the world. Over eighty percent of people who invest in a self-help, inspirational or motivational product never get past the first chapter. Now I want you to join the guys in the top 5% who actually take what they have heard and implement it into their life.

Secret 6 - The Good News

"I believe in God, but not as one thing, not as an old man in the sky. I believe that what people call God is something in all of us. I believe that what Jesus and Mohammed and Buddha and all the rest said was right. It's just that the translations have gone wrong", John Lennon

My intention for this book is to change your life. A dramatic statement that almost certainly is hugely over used and casually thrown out by authors without any consideration to whether the material has any real power to live up to that grand claim. 'Life changing' has become just another sales statement in most cases but I believe that the essential concept of this book carries the ultimate paradigm shift to alter every aspect of your life on earth.

I have hinted and tip toed around the issue until this point because if I had gone ahead and blurted out the central concept of this book at the very beginning you would have pigeon holed me as an eccentric British nut job... Who knows perhaps that is exactly what I am? The only evidence I can offer the skeptics is, what I am telling you about in this book has dramatically changed my life for the better. The principles of manifestation I followed and are now sharing with you took me from being an alcoholic, broke and broken shambles of a man to a sober, deeply happy and contented individual living with his soul mate in an environment of pure love and abundance.

Stop beating around the bush Craig, I hear you cry. Earlier I told you that we are all a fragment of God. If you imagine an infinite sheet of ice that exploded into seven billion pieces and in every one of us is embedded a sliver of this divine material. If you were open-minded enough to swallow that incomprehensible morsel, I now want to take that idea further. You see, this concept is a bit of an illusion; it's a dilution of the truth to help more people accept a tricky and somewhat counter intuitive concept. By stating that you have a fragment of God inside you implies that there are parts of you that are not divine, parts of you that are disconnected from source. The 'fragment' concept is only a slight of hand; it is ultimately flawed as a principle because it takes us straight back to the illusion of separation that we talked about earlier. Despite the variety of senses, sights, sounds and experiences here on earth everything is just another expression of God.

You are God, and so am I.

Let me say that again because that one sentence changes everything. You are God and so am I, so is your partner, so are your children and so is everything you see around you. Not many can instantly accept this concept and if you are currently raising a suspicious eyebrow in my direction, just pause your quizzical mind for a moment and consider what would happen to racism, vanity and jealousy if we all knew for certain that we are in fact God.

Nobody on earth could be any better or worse than you, we are all the same. Being jealous of another person is a pointless waste of time, it makes no more sense than your right foot being envious of your left foot.

I am blessed with two wonderful and amazing children, a little girl called Aoife who is 15, and I can't believe Jordan, the little boy I used to bounce on my knee is now a 18 year old, six foot tall wide receiver with a six pack and defined muscles I never had even in the prime of my youth. I try my best not to stand next to him these days. They are both perfectly healthy and happy with excellent eyesight and hearing. I make reference to their auditory health because something strange happens at certain times of day. When I shout upstairs and tell my kids to turn off the television and get some sleep their hearing is worryingly poor, in fact I would describe them as being completely and profoundly deaf. I am pretty sure it's nothing to do with the acoustics of our home, because when I whisper to my partner that we should maybe order in pizza for the night they are downstairs and salivating like Pavlov's dogs before I have finished the sentence.

My kids are not the only ones with this selective hearing. We are all extremely talented and diligent information cherry pickers. Within us is a clear path to happiness, but more often than not we simply choose not to listen. A good physical world analogy would be like carrying around the winning lottery numbers in your handbag but making the decision never to play them. Then having opted out of the competition getting annoyed and upset because you are still not as wealthy as you want to be.

By choosing to listen to the insane demands of our ego and by ignoring the voice of our soul we all make happiness preventing decisions on a daily basis. The ego makes predictions of the future, based on events of the past; it speculates that what has gone before is likely to happen again. If you were brought up in a family that believed that money was hard to come by and that wealth was the trappings of the evil rich (other people) and not the everyday man, then your ego will predict that there will be more of the same in the future. Life becomes one big self-fulfilling prophecy, is it not true that overweight parents often bring up overweight children, who go on to struggle with their weight for the rest of their lives?

Because everything created by the ego will have been born out of the raw emotion of fear, it will have significant aspects to it that are incorrect.

For example, you may believe that your friend James is tight with money and never pays his fair share when you are socializing together. This is a subjective opinion of your ego based on your own attachment to and fear of losing material possessions. Your ego worries that if you are spending more than your fair share on other people, there might not be enough left for you; after all, money is hard to come by, right? You are making judgments without having access to the full facts. The reality of James' spending habits are unknown, he could be saving money to pay for his old mum's operation, or he could indeed just have an ego equally pessimistic about money as you do. Who knows, or cares? The truth is irrelevant and makes no difference to the point I am making here.

This opinion of the ego is always a "Secondary Thought Event', in other words, whilst you come to these judgments in the blink of an eye, faster than any modern day computer, they still cross the finishing line into your mind in a clear second place. There is a thought that comes half a second before these opinions, and this is what I call 'The Primary Thought Event (PTE)'.

Normally PTE's happen around questions of integrity and so you are unlikely to feel their presence whilst trying to decide what flavor ice cream to buy at the movie theatre, or which pair of shoes to wear on a night out at an expensive restaurant. However, in circumstances of merit this voice resonates throughout your body with clear direction as to what you should do. Actually it is never a voice but rather a feeling and they are easy to identify. But the problem is you never get much chance to analyze the sensation and be fully aware of what it is. The ego is in high pursuit behind the PTE and will arrive in your mind within half a second. In most cases the first thing your ego will do is to try and prevent you taking any action based on that primary thought. It strongly and convincingly argues that you should ignore the primary thought event completely.

Why does the conscious fear this voice so much? Because it shatters the illusion that the ego has spent a lifetime trying to convince you is real. The ego hates any reminder that it is not in control of your destiny. The

Primary Thought Event is the voice of your soul. It comes from a position of pure love and is blessed with the knowledge and understanding of what this life is all about. It knows that you have nothing to lose and it knows there is no such thing as death. It knows what is best for you and given half the chance it would steer you on the path that serves you best. However, the ego will fight hard to prevent this disaster from happening because it knows this source has no attachment to anything material. It is highly likely to suggest you give away a raft of things your ego has spent many years persuading you to acquire.

Your conscious mind will tell you that your home is your castle and nobody can take it off you. It will tell you that you have a better car than your neighbor and as such must be more successful. The ego will tell you that your marriage will last forever and a million other things that hint at permanency being possible. It does this not for your benefit but out of an insane drive to defy the unbreakable law of mortality. It tries to build a world where things can last forever in the hope that if it can make that concept true then it will one day also be able to avoid the inevitable.

Let me paint a picture for you, a typical example of the PTE being ignored... A city worker pushed open the thick glass door of his air-conditioned office and walked out into the warm muggy air of the busy street. His expensive suit cuts him a fine and respectable figure as he walks to the nearby deli to pick up a sandwich and orange juice for his lunch. On route, no more than fifty meters from his office door, he spots a young man slumped on the floor begging for loose change. He must be no more than 19 years old, his clothes are dirty and torn and he has an expression of hopelessness etched into his young face. He is not bothering people, just simply holding out a scrawny, limp and defeated hand for any coins. BANG! A PTE happens that clearly says 'give the man money, give him lots of money', it says to the city gent 'you have plenty, even if you emptied all the notes from your wallet it wouldn't make any difference you would just refill the wallet from the abundance that you have'. This opinion represents who you are at a divine level, it is the voice of your soul, or if you want a more grandiose statement, this is the voice of God. Less than half a second later his ego goes into panic at the thought that he might actually be considering 'giving this person all our money'.

The ego, with a scarcity mindset, has alarm bells ringing all over the place and it begins to argue that it would be ridiculous to give all the money to this man, because then there wouldn't be enough left to buy lunch. As he gets closer to the homeless man, his mind is in turmoil. He feels that he should give the man money but can't argue against the strong position of the conscious mind. The ego suggests a compromise; maybe just a few coins would be better and more appropriate than the folding stuff. Desperately the man hunts in his pocket for loose change. He can't find any and his ego advises to avoid looking bad he simply crosses the road to skip the situation altogether.

So the man crosses the road and continues his journey to the sandwich shop, the down and out who really needed the money got nothing, and the gentleman who was talked out of responding to the PTE lost the opportunity to experience the joy of giving to another and flowing in the same direction as his soul.

Did the city worker do a bad thing? No. As we have previously stated, good and bad are always subjective, the homeless man may have used that money to clean himself up and eat a decent meal, or he could just have likely spent it on alcohol or hard drugs. No act is either good or bad, but rather it is a decision that either serves us or it doesn't serve us.

When you follow the PTE you allow perfection to flow into your life, it's the gift that keeps giving. The person you helped benefits (although this is almost irrelevant), you also benefit by doing something that 'serves you' and your act of selecting to permit divinity to act in defiance of the ego causes disruption to the power of the conscious mind. Every time the ego is prevented from controlling your response to life's events, it gets a fraction of a percent weaker as a result.

Do this often enough, and the effect on your ego is compounded; slowly you start trusting your thoughts less and start acting in flow with God more.

"By night even atheists half believe", Edward Young

The law of attraction is not a new concept; it predates all religions just as all our other laws did. Recently the concept of 'manifesting', 'cosmic ordering' and 'attraction' have entered the mainstream vocabulary but they are just trendy labels for something that man has been doing since the dawn of creation, wishing and praying. Manifesting is just the same as praying with certainty.

Perhaps we wouldn't even need books like this one if religion hadn't painted the image of God as the bearded angry guy who sits on a throne passing judgment on us sinful mortals. As a whole, we seem to have got terribly mixed up about praying. More often than not we drop to our knees and ask God for help only in our darkest moments. We see prayer as a cry for help, like a child who has fallen off the swing screams for his mother. What upsets us with prayer is when we fall off the swing and 'mom' doesn't come running. Our cries for help appear to go unnoticed, and this causes us a great sensation of being alone and unloved.

When traumatic events happen to us we ask what we believe to be entirely reasonable things of a God, who is supposed to care beyond all others. In the darkest of moments we beg that God makes the cancer go away or grants us enough luck to keep the business afloat for just another week. Whatever it is, these prayers are born of desperation and are unlikely to result in the outcome we desire. When the family member dies and the business goes under we feel abandoned by God. We look to the heavens and wonder why he chose to ignore us in our darkest moment. We want to ask why our prayer wasn't answered but are faced with nothing but silence.

Religion has burdened us with guilt and the belief that we don't even deserve the things we are praying for. Even as we look to the heavens and beg for God to intervene and save us or our loved one for the most part we don't believe we will get what we so desperately need because we are worthless in the eyes of God, condemned by our impure thoughts, greed and lust.

The reality is every prayer is answered, it's just that sometimes the answer is no and at other times it is a qualified yes, 'as in not now but later'. When most people drop to their knees and ask God for something and they don't get the response they want, they make the assumption that God either did not hear, chose to ignore the prayer, or worse still, that God does not even exist. Here is the hardest truth to swallow, if your prayer didn't work it was you who created that response, you are God and you answer your own prayers.

I am hoping that you can now see that the traditional view of God sitting on a glorious and opulent throne in the heavens is childish nonsense. God is not a person and as such cannot be accused of displaying any sort of human behavior. God did not ignore the prayer or choose to let the individual suffer. The very suggestion of such actions insinuates that we are back at the image of a vengeful deity who is separate from us. A God who sits in judgment of our sins on earth, handing out rewards and punishment accordingly.

We must keep reminding ourselves that both time and the illusion of separation are not real. God exists within you; he is embedded inside you as that fragment we talked about earlier.

If you are God and God is you… then where do you think your prayers should be addressed?

That's right you have the power to grant your own prayers. That does not mean you can decide to win the lottery tomorrow or go around healing the sick. Remember all these desires to own things, be more successful, achieve greater wealth and be faster, bigger, slimmer or better than other people are just the insane ramblings of your ego. Do you not think that the divine part of you can tell the source of these material demands and chose to ignore them in your best interests? Equally do you really have to doubt whether the fragment of God within you knows what is best for you, even before you ask?

Your soul not only knows what is best for you but it wants to give it to you. A lifetime of blissful happiness is lined up for you, if you would just let go of the illusion that you are in control of life. For most of your time on this earth you have struggled to swim up stream, determined to get to something you have decided you need to be happy. I am here to tell you that if you just stop kicking and struggling then all you could ever need is waiting for you down stream, where the river wants to take you.

You would think if we are meant to pray and then it should be easy for anyone to do. This is true but then everything is easy once you know how. Riding a bicycle is easy if you know how to do it, right? But when you first try to get on one and ride, did you not fall flat on your face? Initially you could stay on that thing for more than a couple of seconds before tumbling off and collecting a few cuts and bruises on the way. Eventually your dad probably fitted training wheels to that bike so you wouldn't get discouraged. Once your confidence had grown and more importantly you believed you could really ride the bike, he took the stabilizers off and set you on your way with a helping push.

Manifesting through prayer is no different; it is a simple thing to do when you know how. The difference is, hardly anyone stops you when you are getting it wrong and puts your training wheels on for a while.

When most people pray for something they kneel, close their eyes and direct their thoughts upwards to the heavens. They say something like *"God, please help me pay the bills this month, we work very hard and when payday comes there is still not enough money to make ends meet. Make this month better than last month and allow something to happen so we have enough to get by. If you can do that for me I promise I will come to church more often / give to charity more / be a better person"* etc, etc.

A month later and the bills remain unpaid, the person feels his prayer was ignored and then the ego kicks in again with the usual nonsense of 'God must be punishing me'. Why do we find it easier to assume that God is angry with us than that he didn't hear it in the first place? In reality, that person answered their own prayer, but they didn't get the outcome they wanted because they placed the request in the future. This person stated that the present moment is bad and the future will be better. Only the ego operates in the past and in the future; the soul and God work only in the present.

Any prayers set in the future are destined to fail because it is only a statement of the ego and nothing more. Prayers are answered by your soul, the fragment of God operating in blissful ignorance of the past and future. Ask your soul for a lottery win this weekend and you will get nothing in return. This weekend does not exist in the eyes of your soul. The only thing that exists from the point of view of God is this precise moment. To become a creator of your destiny rather than someone who reacts to the life that has been forced upon them, you need to see the beauty in every moment and be grateful for it.

Think about this moment now, what is amazing in your life now? If your automatic answer is 'nothing, my life sucks at the moment', you are not trying hard enough. Spend a few moments thinking about what is really special in your life now.

Let me give you an example of how you can choose to focus on the negative and make your prayers based on that. At the moment I know that I feel sad because I don't get to see my family enough, because my work takes me around the world. I feel a little guilty that I don't get to be the hands on father that I dreamt I would be because I am away on business so often. I know there is big tax demand on the way and I am not looking forward to paying that… I could go on and on. Then I could drop to my knees and say '*God, please let me spend more time with my family and help me pay the tax demand*' etc, etc. This prayer will not work, or perhaps more accurately I should say, this prayer would not give me the outcome I desire.

All that prayer will deliver is more of what I have focused on in the moment that I offered it. In that precise moment I had 'sadness', 'guilt' and 'worry' on offer, and that is exactly what I will get more of as a result. Your soul is a divine creator, a manifestation weapon of limitless power, but with the safety switch off… be careful where you point that thing, it might go off! Aim it at the negative and it will create more negatives (free will is a pain, right?), but aim it at the positive and guess what happens?

So, let's talk about me again (my ego will love this), but instead of thinking about the lack of time I got to spend at home last month, or that big bill that is coming next month, let's stay in this precise moment and build a prayer based on that.

Right now I am so grateful that I am sharing this knowledge with you, I know that these words resonate with me at a very deep level and I am excited about the impact they might make to kindred spirits around the world. I have two stunningly amazing children who I love with all my heart. I have someone special in my life that loves me very much. I have food, shelter, safety and all the other basic requirements of life. It's 7.15am and I am sitting at my desk listening to the soft summer rain outside, today is a blank canvas and I am grateful for the world of opportunities available to me.

Wow, suddenly I feel good… I really encourage you to do the same task, and do it now. Don't let your ego make a promise that you will do this later, grab a piece of paper and start writing now. Scribble down all the amazing things in your life, ignore the stuff that has gone before and avoid the shoulda, woulda, coulda's.

As we have already discovered; your conscious desires and wants are an irrelevance, so forget about what you think you want. These dreams are all in the tomorrow and none of your business. Concentrate on what is in your life today, this moment, and be grateful for it. Even problems present as an opportunity for love and gratitude. Give your problems to God, ask God to erase them and then give thanks for that.

I think Marelisa Fabrega describes it best in her change blog when she says:

Gratitude means thankfulness, counting your blessings, noticing simple pleasures, and acknowledging everything that you receive. It means learning to live your life as if everything were a miracle, and being aware on a continuous basis of how much you've been given.

Gratitude shifts your focus from what your life lacks to the abundance that is already present. In addition, behavioural and psychological research has shown surprising life improvements that can stem from the practice of gratitude. Giving thanks makes people happier and more resilient, it strengthens relationships, it improves health, and it reduces stress.

Two psychologists, Michael McCollough of Southern Methodist University in Dallas, Texas, and Robert Emmons of the University of California at Davis, wrote an article about an experiment they conducted on gratitude and its impact on well-being. The study split several hundred people into three different groups and all of the participants were asked to keep daily diaries. The first group kept a diary of the events that occurred during the day without being told specifically to write about either good or bad things; the second group was told to record their unpleasant experiences; and the last group was instructed to make a daily list of things for which they were grateful. The results of the study indicated that daily gratitude exercises resulted in higher reported levels of alertness, enthusiasm, determination, optimism, and energy. In addition, those in the **gratitude** group experienced less depression and stress, were more likely to help others, exercised more regularly, and made greater progress toward achieving personal goals.

People tend to take for granted the good that is already present in their lives. There's a gratitude exercise that instructs that you should imagine losing some of the things that you take for granted, such as your home, your ability to see or hear, your ability to walk, or anything that currently gives you comfort. Then imagine getting each of these things back, one by one, and consider how grateful you would be for each and every one. In addition, you need to start finding joy in the small things instead of holding out for big achievements—such as getting the promotion, having a comfortable nest egg saved up, getting married, having the baby, and so on–before allowing yourself to feel gratitude and joy.

Another way to use giving thanks to appreciate life more fully is to use gratitude to help you put things in their proper perspective. When things don't go your way, remember that every difficulty carries within it the seeds of an equal or greater benefit. In the face of adversity ask yourself: "What's good about this?", "What can I learn from this?", and "How can I benefit from this?"

Once you become oriented toward looking for things to be grateful for, you will find that you begin to appreciate simple pleasures and things that you previously took for granted. Gratitude should not be just a reaction to getting what you want, but an all-the-time gratitude, the kind where you notice the little things and where you constantly look for the good, even in unpleasant situations. Today, start bringing gratitude to your experiences, instead of waiting for a positive experience in order to feel grateful; in this way, you'll be on your way toward becoming a master of gratitude.

And here is the final but most magical piece of information I have learned, how to get your prayers answered every time. Be the outcome you desire; it really is as simple as that. Want to be wealthy? Then act wealthy, be grateful for the wealth that you have, even if you have nothing but a few coins in your pocket, be grateful for them. Instead of thinking about yesterday when you had ten coins or predicting that by tomorrow you will have none, stay in the moment of now and love the fact that you have money.

Act like you have money, I don't mean go waste it on desires of your ego, but give it away if the Primary Thought Events tells you that's what you should do. When you give away something the subconscious assumes you must have plenty and so it works to create that reality. Who would have thought that giving away money creates more money?

Hey, and you know what, it works with everything; want more love? Then give more love! But remember that the (free will) safety switch is always turned off, give away abuse and negativity and guess what your life gets more of?

Whether you arrived at this book due to a mid life crisis (I have had several of those babies) or the burning question of 'why' has always lingered at the back of your mind I hope this book has given you some answers. If not completely relieving the itch, then perhaps allowing some relief by virtue of the knowledge that you are not alone with these thoughts.

As I stated right at the very start of this book, I do not claim that what I believe is the only way. I have no way of proving anything I have said here in this series, all I know is that as a result of discovering this knowledge I am more at peace now, than I have ever been. I write this book in the sincere hope that you too find the same tranquility as a result of reading this material. Whether I am right or not, whether heaven exists or we simply come back and do the whole thing over into infinity, it makes no odds to this moment in time. Above all else, what I have learned is this:

If you want to be sad, then live in the past.
If you want to feel worried, then live in the future.
If you want to be happy then live in the now.

Whether you are Christian, Muslim, Jewish, Agnostic or Atheist the beautiful thing is the point of life is the same for all. Love is what is all about, the reason for you and me to exist is simply contained within one four-letter word; LOVE! I don't just mean for your husband, wife, boyfriend or girlfriend but rather every aspect of life. If every area of your existence is directed by your passion for it then you will experience a peace and contentment beyond your wildest dreams. Follow the primary thought event, because deep inside you there is a Fragment of Perfect Love, just bursting to share its power with everyone and every thing that comes into your life.

If you don't get up each morning and sprint to work because you love every minute of it, then what the hell are you doing it for? Don't tell me it's for the money because that fragment inside you doesn't care about money, if you really want more it will create more – but only if what you are doing comes with all the passion you can muster. Look around the world and study the richest people on the planet, are they rich because they work harder than everyone else? Not a chance, I bet you will discover that most of them are wealthy as a result of doing what they are passionate about.

I started this Manifesting Magic series talking about attracting more money, simply because it's the common starting place for people on this journey. Forget about money, it's purely the by-product of doing what you love. If you follow your heart and have fun creating stuff, money flows into your life as an automatic consequence of your actions.

In the final part of this seven volume series I will give you the tools to put the whole jigsaw together. Over six concise books I have shown you the secrets to more wealth, better health, amazing relationships, career success and spiritual balance. You have all the components of a dream life. However, at the moment it's a bit like being given all 2.3 million parts required to build a Boeing 787, just because you have everything you need doesn't mean you own a Dreamliner.

I hope you have arrived at this place in sequence, starting with part one and working through in order to reach this the end point of part 6. If you have skipped any sections of the Manifesting Magic series now is the time to go back and fill in the gaps. This is important to do before you move on to the final and most powerful stage in the course. In Manifesting Magic part seven I will be showing you how to make it all automatic. Implement what I tell you and allow it to permeate deeply into your subconscious mind. When you get to this point true magic will start appearing in your life. If your heart desires something it will appear.

I do sincerely hope that you know by now that none of this about bragging or keeping up with the Jones's. I am telling you here and now that I am the richest man on planet earth, but that statement has nothing to do with money. I have everything that my heart desires; I live in the sunshine on a small island in the Mediterranean Sea. I share my life with my soul mate and our little zoo of animals that we rescued along the way. Two cheeky dogs called Contessa and Laika and two elegant if somewhat needy cats called Junior and Mishu. This is the life I would of (and did) designed for myself. To you it may not sound all that great, perhaps your perfect world would include a penthouse apartment overlooking the alps or a farm with acres of open space but to me it is heaven on earth. It doesn't matter where you are starting from you too can build the life you really desire. Your success at this law of attraction business has nothing to do with intelligence, luck or geography. You can start with nothing in any location and situation you care to think of and still reach the heights of your imagination.

Secret 7 – Inside The Vortex

A few years ago, the city council of Monza, Italy, barred pet owners from keeping goldfish in curved bowls... saying that it is cruel to keep a fish in a bowl with curved sides because, gazing out, the fish would have a distorted view of reality. But how do we know we have the true, undistorted picture of reality", Stephen Hawking

Let us start with the premise that inside each one of us is a divine particle of source. A perfect morsel of the universe that wants for nothing, needs nothing and desires nothing. This part of you consists of one emotion and one emotion only, love. It is acutely aware that it is eternal and that it is one with everything else. It has no fear of death and knows precisely why you are here and what you need to find your own happiness, peace and purpose on earth. This part of you not only knows what your heart desires but it also knows exactly how to give it to you. It is only reasonable for you to wonder then; why do you still not have the life you want?

The reason you still feel that emptiness inside you is because you are currently blocking all the divine elements from entering your life. It's similar to trying to pour yourself a glass of soda with the bottle cap only half loosened. The soda drips into the glass, but not quickly enough to give you anything worthwhile. In the case of the law of attraction and manifesting the life of your dreams, it is not a bottle cap preventing the outcome you desire but seven universal illusions that stop you from seeing what needs to be done to restore the flow. In this final section of Manifesting Magic, I am going to remind you what the illusions are and show you how to fine-tune your thinking and behavior to permit this powerful life changing force to rush into your life.

If you are wondering why there are seven universal laws, haven't you noticed that it's always seven? Stephen Covey wrote about the seven habits of highly successful people, there were seven brides for the seven brothers and there are seven books in the Manifesting Magic series.

The Seven Illusions:

1. **The illusion of separation**

    This first common blockage is centered on the assumption that what we see happening before our eyes is really as it appears! A belief that we are all entirely self-sufficient individuals with no significant connection to anyone who falls outside the circle of our immediate family and friends. Falling for this illusion is like the branches of a tree believing that they have nothing to do with each other.

    When we strip everything down to its atomic level, there is no difference between any of us. We are not just similar: we are made of the exact same material, the same as every other life form or physical object on earth. We are composed of particles of energy vibrating in an infinite variety of frequencies. You can already see how removing this one blockage from the human condition would effectively render racism, sexism and any other *ism* you can think of impossible in one fell swoop.

This illusion forces us to ignore the divinity within us and listen only to the insane ramblings of the ego. This act pushes our vibrational frequency lower and further away from where we need to be to start attracting the life we really desire.

2. **The illusion of God**

Religion has made quite a few monumentally flawed assumptions about who, what and where God is. Over many thousands of years, traditional religion has taken certain commonly agreed upon facts and leapt to various spurious postulations. One of which is that God is perfect and therefore we are all a pale reflection of his majesty. A species he created from dirt and is a constant sinful disappointment to him (for God is a man, don't you know?).

The Christian concept of original sin implies that even the newborn baby is doomed to play this depressing role for his or her entire life. But don't go thinking that death will bring a release from this condemnation. Their only hope of avoiding an eternity in the fiery pit of hell is to spend this lifetime on their knees begging an angry God for forgiveness (forgiveness for things it hasn't even done). No wonder church attendances are in perpetual decline.

Let's be grown up about this; God is not the old man sitting on a cloud passing judgment on us. God is within us, a part of our being. Essentially, we are God and God is us, and accepting this crucial principle allows divinity to flow from within us. Ironically, to even state such a thing is also considered a mortal sin in itself by traditional religions. So if you tell your priest about this book, you are 99% guaranteed to piss off the big man upstairs.

3. **The illusion of labels**

We tend to describe God as being a man and perhaps even picture him as having human physical form. God is not a person and has no other earthly construct. There is no height, depth, size or shape to God. God has no gender, face, hair, legs or arms. God does not reside anywhere but rather everywhere. The word God is just a label to help children apply a simple context to a principle that is confusing and beyond the comprehension of even our brightest thinkers.

The problem with labels is that they come with baggage. If I tell you to pray, you may refuse because you are not religious. However, manifesting and cosmic ordering are just other labels that mean the same thing as prayer. We tend to get wrapped up in the labels of life. If someone claims we are dishonest, we get very offended, even if it's not true.

You may think initially that positive labels are a benefit. For example it would be entirely reasonable to assume that having a reputation for being a good parent, kind nurse, dedicated son or generous friend are all positive badges for someone to wear. The label itself is not the problem but our attachment to them as some sort of false God.

Here's an extreme example for you. If I wrote a book about what a bitch Mother Teresa was, then a lot of people would get very offended and immediately jump to her defense. They would insult me and refer me to the huge amount of selfless work that she did to help others as proof that she is worthy of all the positive labels we collectively adorn her memory with. People would attack the insult because they feel attached to and secure in their beliefs about Mother Teresa.

Nobody likes to have their beliefs stolen from them, even if they are not beliefs that serve any sort of positive purpose. Millions of people around the world drink to near alcoholic levels because they believe that booze is a harmless social pleasantry. They choose to ignore the fact that alcohol is a registered poison and in the early nineties was proven beyond reasonable doubt to be a leading cause of cancer. They like their beliefs (their beliefs give them permission to drink) and they do not want to be reminded that 3.5 million people die every year as a direct result of drinking alcohol. A lot of them will get very offended if you challenge their drinking or criticize their drug (by the way, they also don't like it being called a drug).

Before we leap to the defense of Mother Teresa and her treatment at the pen of this terrible, unscrupulous author, we should ask some important questions:

- Do my insults take anything away from the amazing work she did?
- Do my claims change who she was as a person?
- Am I correct in my assertion?

If the answer to all those questions is no, then why do we waste so much energy getting angry? Shortly you will find out just how powerful that energy is, and it will confirm for you once and for all that it should never be wasted on negative pursuits such as this.

To remove the blockage caused by this third illusion, try to detach yourself from giving yourself or other people and events around you specific labels. The law of attraction works by altering your own vibrational energy to match that of the universal field of energy that flows through everything else. You can label this field God/Source/Cosmos/The Universe or Dave: it doesn't make any difference. If I call you a thief, you don't instantly become a thief as a consequence of my action, and this powerful field of energy doesn't change based on what you call it either.

4. The illusion of time

This is a tricky one to accept, but time as we generally refer to it in day-to-day life does not really exist. Time implies something linear exists in our world, a bit like watching a movie on one of those old VHS videotapes. When you insert the tape into the machine and press *play*, you watch the pre-recorded events unfold. The end of the movie already exists and if you so choose you can fast-forward the tape to a future point. Equally, if you miss a bit of the action, you can hit the rewind button and go back in 'time'. Life appears to be similar to the format of a VHS videotape because we can remember the past and we assume that there will also be a future.

However, we cannot rewind life because what happened before this precise moment does not exist anymore. We cannot fast-forward life through the bad points because the future does not exist either. If VHS movies were actually like real life, then the tape would be blank when you inserted it in the machine. The machine would create the story appearing on the screen at the moment you viewed it and then instantly erase it as soon as the image leaves the screen. At the end of the movie, the videotape would once again be completely blank.

The past and the future are virtual creations of our ego and nothing more. Everything is happening now, in this moment, and only in this moment. We have no fast-forward and no rewind buttons.

When we forget that time is just an illusion, we start trying to control aspects of reality that simply don't exist. We hope for a better future, we dream about reliving the glorious victories of our youth. These wishes will never be fulfilled because they are all located in a time period that will never be. This is not something new to people trying out the law of attraction or cosmic ordering. For thousands of years, people have been praying to God and all the time placing their requests in a time period that doesn't exist. They ask to win the lottery on Saturday, to be able to pay the bills next month or for something as general as for life to be better in the future.

When I was a child, my parents used to regularly take me and my brother to a country pub in the North East of England called the A1 (named after the famous road on which it was situated). Above the bar was a polished brass sign; it said 'All drinks free tomorrow'. Of course, the comedy being that if you come back tomorrow the sign will still say the same thing. Tomorrow and yesterday do not exist in this moment and nobody ever got a free pint of beer in that pub.

I appreciate that this illusion is the most complicated one to accept because it defies everything we have seen unfold before us. We start at birth and we struggle through life as long as we possibly can until eventually we die. It's hard to deny this is the reality because we have seen many people be born, live and then eventually pop their clogs, as the saying goes. Purely from the point of view of using the law of attraction, it is much more helpful to see this as nothing more than an illusion. The fact that you were alive yesterday and you may also be alive tomorrow has no relevance to what happens to you right here in this moment (the only moment that will ever exist). The unseen reality is that you are more like a creator choosing to manifest life second by second. Every moment that appears, you create and then destroy instantly. You do this millions of times over a lifetime.

If it makes it easier, try to view your time on earth as a period in which you experience thousands of different lives. Each day represents a new life, a new opportunity to manifest. Today cannot touch yesterday or tomorrow. It is only valid for 24 hours. Think about this: tonight you will go to sleep and while you are dreaming, your central nervous system will destroy, discard and replace millions of cells in your body. By the time you wake up tomorrow morning, a percentage of who you were today will have disappeared forever and a similar percentage of you will be taking its first ever step on planet earth in the role of you. Fast forward a few months and virtually every part of the 'you' that exists today will be gone, replaced by entirely new cells.

Let go of the past. You were not there anyway. Forget about the future. You will never get there either.

5. The illusion of scarcity

As a species we struggle with this. We even teach our children that money is hard to come by and should be saved for a rainy day. It would be better if we looked at money like water. It flows all over the planet and everywhere it goes it's useful, it makes things happen and it's passed along. We could say that water doesn't belong to any of us or that it belongs to all of us. When water is flowing and moving, it cleanses, it purifies, it makes things green, it creates growth, it nurtures. But when water starts to slow down, is held back and starts to be still, it can be toxic and stagnant to those who hold it.

Many believe that you are a better person if you are poor and that if you become rich, you also become greedy and unclean at the same time. The truth is, money doesn't really exist. Money is just traded for power and it is power that we believe corrupts, as the saying goes.

The desire for money and power comes only from fear, and fear is purely a construct of your ego. The fragment of divinity within you is not afraid of anything. Think about it, why would God be afraid of not having a car as extravagant as his neighbor's, who is also God?

Living in a scarcity mindset is a powerful block to the law of attraction and ultimately to you living a happy, peaceful and fulfilling life on earth.

6. The illusion of blame

Any excuse for your misery that points the finger of blame at someone else is a block to manifestation. Claiming you are hopeless in relationships because your parents never showed you any love as a child may or may not be true, but the act of holding onto the blame is the action that is causing you problems today.

Holding on to resentment is like holding onto a red-hot stone with the intention of throwing it at the person you blame. You are the one who gets burnt.

"You must take private responsibility. You can notice the circumstances, the seasons nor the wind does change, only you yourself can change"
~ Jim Rohn

The most widespread misconception in contemporary times is that we firmly believe that we have a right to a fantastic, perfect life. Increasingly, we are breeding generations that are cursed with a terrible sense of entitlement. That somehow, somewhere, someone (definitely not us) enriches our lives with constant joy, interesting careers, fantastic options and a chilled family life in addition to joyous personal partnerships that only exist because we exist.

Is it not true that your parents think you are lucky because you had so much more than they did when they were growing up? If you have children, you probably now witness the same evolution of materialism unfolding again. The collective ego of the world is snowballing as our children watch the super-rich on TV every week. I am pretty sure that my daughter thinks that the Kardashians represent real life and her cruel parents are deliberately exposing her to relative poverty just to be mean.

The life you want will never be found in an external location, nor will it be delivered to you on a silver plate. The reality is that there is just one person who is accountable for the quality of your life.

That person is YOU.

If you want to succeed and accomplish your intentions, you need to take 100% responsibility for everything that happens in your life. This includes your level of efficiency, the results you generate, the quality of your relationships, your state of health and wellness and physical fitness, your salary, your debts, your emotions—everything!

The majority of us have been so conditioned, however, that we blame everybody, anything beyond our own selves for the factors in our lives that are not good. We blame our moms and dads, our educators, our boss, the Internet, our partners, the weather, politics or economics. Does pointing the finger of blame change anything in your life? Absolutely nothing. Therefore, the only thing you need to do, if you want to transform something in your life, is to take 100% responsibility for it and your feeling about it. There is no other approach.

I found the following simple formula by Jack Canfield:

E + R= O
Event + Response = Outcome

The idea is that each outcome is determined by the activity and the response. It does not matter if the outcome is success or failure, riches or scarcity, health or sickness, fun or frustration. If you believe the outcome is bad, there are only two possibilities:

A: You can choose to give the event the 'blame' for the lack of results.

Simply put, you can blame everybody: your partner, your children, the general public, your boss and the incompetence of the government or the lack of encouragement you get from your family. These factors exist, no question, but if these were the determining factors in whether you succeed or fail, then nobody would be wealthy.

Bill Gates would never have established Microsoft. Steve Jobs never would have set the mega-corporation Apple rolling down the hill. Do you really think millionaires are just people who grew up with perfect parents and 100% support and encouragement? Gates and Jobs definitely have had the same conditions and became hugely successful nonetheless. You can join them, if you take responsibility.

Blaming others effectively sets yourself limitations about what you believe you can achieve. Remember, 'whether you believe you can or you believe you can't—you are right'. Apportioning blame means that you are giving up or maybe even that you are afraid of success. Lots of people leave the so-called limiting factors behind them, so it cannot be the variables that limit you. The reasons on the outside are not the ones keeping you beyond success; it is always YOU and what you believe about yourself.

We defend ourselves from responsibility even for self-destructive habits (like cigarette smoking and alcohol consumption) with inexcusable reasoning. We tell ourselves that we deserve a nice glass (or more often a bottle) of wine at the end of the day because we have worked hard. Treating ourselves to a carcinogenic glass of poison as a reward for hard work is complete insanity, but we have become so good at avoiding the truth that we can no longer see what is in front of our face.

7. The illusion of assumption

If a tree falls in a forest and there is nobody there to observe it, does it make any sound? Until very recently, my answer to this age-old question would have been *of course it does, don't be so silly*. Only recently, as I have searched for scientific evidence to back up the theories of the law of attraction, has my position changed on this. Not just changed but reversed. I am now more likely to believe that unobserved trees fall in silence. The reasons why are extremely important elements behind the theory of manifestation. I will explain in detail shortly.

Over the centuries, we have become more and more sophisticated as a species. We used to believe the earth was flat because it looked that way. We used to believe the sun revolved around the earth because from our earthly point of view, that seems to be the most logical conclusion and so we made an assumption.

Go back to Roman times or even the ancient Greeks and belief in multiple Gods was common. Today, that is roundly considered a laughably flawed theory, and the single deity has become the default position of Western religions. However, increasingly even this point of view seems too childish a concept for many to accept, and agnosticism and atheism are rapidly growing as the only logical conclusion to be drawn from the facts we are offered. Science is becoming our yardstick, faith is declining and evidence-based belief systems are becoming the mainstream. Seems sensible, right? But where this logic falls over is when we look beyond the surface and start to examine life on a particle-by-particle level.

In quantum physics, we are discovering that the elements don't obey logic and our assumptions are making an ass of you and me. Perhaps the most famous quantum research study that you will hear mentioned is what was called the 'twin slit experiment'.

To describe the twin slit experiment, consider a Ping-Pong ball firing device that shoots out Ping-Pong balls that travel across a space and hit the wall.

Now think of the ball-firing machine being compressed down to the size of the quantum level and rather than shooting out Ping-Pong balls, it now shoots out extremely tiny particles called electrons. Those electrons pass through a vacuum and hit the wall, which marks their positions.

Now picture a small screen with a single vertical slit in the center that is positioned between the particle launcher and the wall. Many of the electrons will travel through the slit and hit the wall behind it and many will be blocked.

What we will see on the wall is a vertical column clearly showing where the electrons have hit the wall (directly behind the slit).

Next, rather than a single slit, imagine the screen contains double slits. Now the electrons can travel through either one of those slits to strike the wall behind the screen.

What we expect to see is two vertical columns marking the region where the electrons pass through on slit or the other and make impact with the wall. But the peculiar and amazing thing is that we do not witness what we assumed would happen. Instead what we see are several vertical columns a small distance apart from one another appearing on the wall.

Imagine a swimming pool partitioned by a screen. This screen has two slits in the center exactly the same as I just described for our lab-based experiment. When an object is dropped into the pool in front of the twin slit partition, it causes a circular wave to ripple outward in every direction. The surge travels through the twin slits and divides into two smaller waves. As the two ripples continue to travel, they simultaneously reinforce and counteract each other at certain angles.

What you observe on the wall at the end are numerous vertical columns, each spread a minimal amount apart from the next. The columns show where the waves bolster one another, while the spaces demonstrate where the waves cancel each other out.

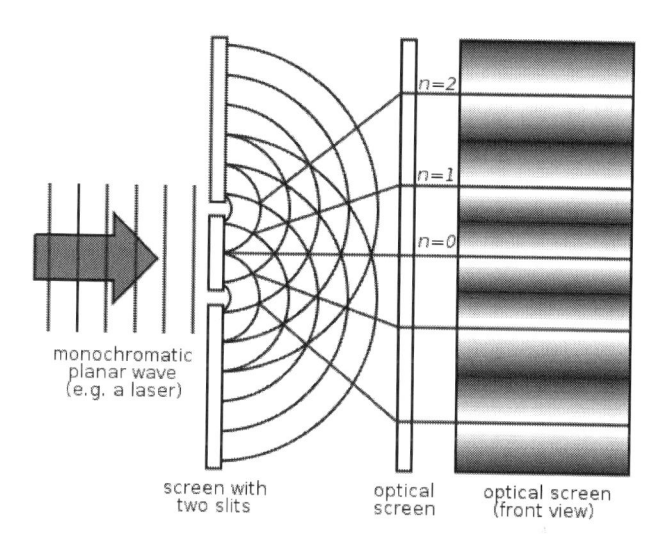

Figure: Double-slit experiment diagram showing monochromatic planar wave (e.g. a laser) passing through a screen with two slits, then an optical screen, producing interference pattern at n=0, n=1, n=2 on the optical screen (front view).

So the question is why does the electron act like a wave when it passes through the double apertures?

The theory is that the electron splits into two when it reaches the screen and travels through both holes at the same time. It then disrupts itself, consequently causing a wave effect that creates the multiple lines on the rear wall. In quantum physics, this is called the theory of non-locality, which is the theory that an element exists in two locations at one time. It is not limited to one place in time and space but it becomes universal.

The scientists were fairly certain in their assumption that the multiple lines were being created by the particles creating a wave. So to confirm their hypothesis a tiny device was positioned in front of the double slits in the screen so that they could observe what occurs when the electron penetrates it.

The outcome they got was unusual beyond ordinary explanation. This time, what they saw on the rear wall was just two vertical columns instead of the multiple ones that they had witnessed initially.

This was a complete head-scratcher for the logically minded scientists because what it showed was that when they were watching, a particle acted like a particle. However, when they were not looking, the particles acted like a wave. The scientists struggled to accept this, because it appeared that 2+2=9.

This is very confusing for scientists but it is a beautiful thing for authors like me. I have witnessed my life being completely turned around by something I know to be real. It is my unwavering belief in the law of attraction that makes it work so well for me. Bully for me, but if I want to use this knowledge to help other people, then it is unrealistic to simply demand that they believe 100% in what I am saying. I appreciate that no matter how much you may want to believe me, there is always going to be an eyebrow raised here or there to certain parts of this phenomenon. At times you are going to think 'this is too good to be true'.

I am excited because the double slit experiment allows me to apply logic to something entirely illogical.

Quantum physicists talk about electrons or events being potential rather than being real physical entities. Nothing is solid but rather a liquid of various potentialities, essentially until somebody looks, and then the looking sort of forces the universe to make a determination about which possibility is going to be realized. All of reality is effectively a limitless quantum field of energy, an ocean of boundless opportunities waiting to transpire.

It sounds impossible, but what I am saying to you really is that I believe the tree makes no sound when it falls unless you are there to make the measurement. Your thoughts are the energy that makes the sound; if you are not present, there is no energy and ergo no sound. When you observe life, you automatically generate thoughts and your thoughts create waves of energy that alter reality. Right at the start of this book I told you that you have the power to manifest the life of your dreams and I hope by now you are starting to get excited that this might actually be a very real and tangible reality.

Consciousness is the fuel that alters energy. All energy is actually consciousness; therefore, it is consciousness guiding itself. The observer is not apart from the observation. The experimenter is not apart from the experiment.

Everything is energy and energy is everything. What this experiment proves is that you are the universe and the universe is you. Without your thoughts and interaction, the universe does not exist. Essentially you have a limited but beautiful choice to make. You can sit back and observe life and thereby send out your submissive observational energy waves and accept what comes back (living a reactionary life—like the vast majority of human beings), or you can decide now to take control of the energy that you are emitting into the universe and start designing the outcome you receive back. The only choice you can't make is to opt out of this process. Whatever thoughts you create are going to have an impact on your life and on the universe as a whole, so why not be in the driver's seat rather than live like most people do, as a mere blindfolded passenger.

It's too good to be true

It was always my intention that *Manifesting Magic* would be a practical book that could be quickly understood and applied to your life. I have tried my best to avoid the author's license to flannel and padding. Whether I have succeeded or not will be entirely subjective, I have no doubt. Shortly, I will give you very clear instructions about how you can start manifesting the life of your dreams. If you are 100% certain that what I have told you so far is true, then feel free to skip ahead to the section entitled 'The 421 Journal'. However, if there are thoughts of 'this all sounds too good to be true' buzzing around your conscious mind, I want to take a moment to address those thoughts now.

I consider myself a relatively intelligent guy with enough street smarts to successfully dodge all scams and scammers that have so far taken me on as a potential mug. I do not believe in fairies, leprechauns, the tooth fairy or Father Christmas. I find most conspiracy theories rather tedious and as such I do not believe 9/11 was anything but a terrorist attack and that the white lines you see in the skies (dubbed chem trails) are the government attempting surreptitiously to poison the common people but rather that they are the simple result of high-temperature exhaust fumes hitting super cold air. My father was a butcher from the North East of England and I consider my heritage to be from a no-nonsense working-class family background. I do not write this sort of material lightly or without pure and total conviction that what I am telling you is true. If my parents were old hippies called Tarquin and Jeminah and we loved nothing more than to spend our summers in the woods dancing around a campfire naked, then I would advise you to take my words with extreme caution.

I do not believe in blind faith. If I am told something, I expect to be able to replicate the results I have been informed about or I will discard the notion. The law of attraction has changed my life beyond all recognition, and I want you to experience the state of bliss that I feel right now. This section of the book is designed to answer the (quite logical) questions of naturally skeptical people everywhere. Sensible, grounded people who really want to believe, but for whom there is just a smattering of 'too good to be true' still lingering. I have tried to answer the most frequent questions I am asked on this subject, but if I miss the element that is most causing you puzzlement, please do email me from the website and I will do my very best to give you a comprehensive answer.

Q1. If the law of attraction is real, why don't I see it happening around me all the time?

You do, but you probably don't currently identify it as the law of attraction at work. There is a perfect example of the universe delivering dreams happening here in England at this very moment. I am writing this section of the book in the business lounge of Manchester Airport on Sunday 1st of May 2016. The city of Manchester is preparing for big crowds to descend on it later this afternoon when the players and fans of Leicester City football club arrive to play a crucial soccer match against the world-famous Manchester United. If you are not a follower of British soccer, let me explain that the Leicester City squad of players have an estimated value of around £31,000,000, a lot of money but peanuts by the standards of some clubs. They will be playing the Manchester United team, whose value is thought to be over £340,000,000. If this were Formula One, it would be like racing Michael Schumacher's Ferrari F2004 against a

Ford Fiesta. If Leicester beat Man United today (and I believe they will), they will win the league, if they lose they will still win the league but it will take another week. Regardless of what happens today, Leicester City will end the season significantly higher up the table than the likes of Manchester United, a team worth over ten times more than them.

If you had placed a bet at the start of the soccer season on this outcome, the bookmakers would have laughed you out of the shop. Odds available for this bet were 5000/1. If you are not familiar with sports gambling, allow me to explain. When odds get over 1000/1, it is the bookmaker quite clearly saying this is not going to happen. For instance, you can probably get odds of 10000/1 that Elvis will be found alive and well and running a fish and chip shop in London. Leicester don't have the best players, they don't have the best coaching staff, they don't have the best training facilities and they don't have anywhere near the financial resources of the other clubs, and yet they will beat every other team in the league this year. I suppose you could claim that Leicester City got lucky and perhaps you could point to two or three games and label it good fortune, but the Premiership season is long and hard. You would have to be pretty convinced of the power of luck to claim that this team were just lucky in all 38 games that they played to reach this point.

Our thoughts have energy and when we deeply believe and focus on our desires, we send out immense and powerful waves of this energy. What do you think happens when 100,000 fans all believe the same thing? This is what we call the collective will and it can move mountains. David killed Goliath because he believed, he saw the victory before it happened and sent the corresponding wave of energy into the ether (or if you want the dumbed down explanation, a miracle happened —thank the Lord).

It is worth being aware that the collective will of society can also create devastatingly bad outcomes. Consider World War II for instance; it is a little too easy to point the entire finger of blame at Adolf Hitler. Realistically, one man could not do that much damage on his own. Most of the German people were largely unaware of the true horrific extent of the atrocities being committed in their names, but there were still enough people willing to build, run or just plain ignore the concentration camps on their doorsteps. Camps similar to Auschwitz, where millions of men, women and children were systematically starved, tortured and murdered.

Adolf Hitler wasn't initially a dictator imposing his will on a helpless nation; the people of the time voted him into power. His hard line resonated with the feelings of the downtrodden majority in the country. Germany had been completely humiliated in the First World War and the punishment handed down by the allied nations brought the Germans to their knees. The country was rendered bankrupt and all hope of recovery was pointless due to heavy fines and debts imposed on the country by the rest of Europe. If the situation hadn't changed dramatically, Germany would have been still paying their debts to the allies well into 1987. The country was in a bitter depression with no jobs and no opportunities, and hyperinflation had made the currency next to worthless. In 1922, a loaf of bread in Germany would have cost you

160 marks. One year later, the same loaf of bread cost 200,000,000,000 marks. You literally couldn't carry all the money to the baker that you would need to buy the bread.

The collective mind-set of the people was that of a deep inner resentment that they were being bullied and harshly treated and it was time to stand up and fight back against the bullies. The result of this miserable national state of mind is written in blood in our history books.

Q2. Why can't I do something simple to prove it works, like placing a winning bet on a sports event?

The problem with this concept as a test is that there are too many unknown variables. Let's take a horse race as an example. Imagine there are six runners and you have put a small bet on horse number five, just to test this law of attraction business. What you don't know is how many other people are betting on the other horses and how many of them are also firing their own rockets of intention into the universe. There might be a guy across town wagering his last penny on horse number 2. He is on his knees begging for a result because anything less than a win is going to mean he can't pay his rent and will lose his home. In this situation, your win would cause him significant harm (and you would never know anything about it). You can't ask the universe to manifest harm to other people because divinity is love and love has nothing to do with the array of negative emotions we experience as a part of the human condition.

The second thing I have noticed is that the universe ignores your insistence on when something arrives. Time as we know it is an irrelevant concept to the cosmos. I have found the universe is very similar to Cypriots; it is not in a rush to do anything—tomorrow is just fine thank you very much. Most of the time when you ask for something, you are completely unaware of all the elements that have to come together to make it happen. I could state my intention that I want to see the earth from space just once in my lifetime. I am sure you can see how this could be possible if the right events happen in the correct order. If I demand that I become an astronaut by this afternoon, I am backing the universe into a corner—it doesn't have the material to work with in order to give me what I want. Remember, your intentions need to be for amazing things that are beneficial (or at the very least, that do no harm) to everyone involved.

Finally, I believe you are communicating via a divine fragment of your eternal being. This part of you knows why you are here and what you really should be doing with your life. If you won one horse race, the chances are good you would place another larger bet, and before long this trivial activity would become your obsession. I am reasonably certain that your purpose in life is not just to teach the bookmaker a lesson or two. Giving you what you want in this case could cause a domino effect that destroys your life. The universe will ignore you if you try to cause harm, even if the harm is only to yourself. Remember, the illusion of separation means that it is not possible to contain the harm only to yourself. The damage you inflict on yourself will create a ripple of negative energy that impact others far and wide.

Q3. If we are as powerful and divine as you say, then why do so many bad things happen and why can't we stop them?

The hitch with this question is that it comes from within the illusion of God. It assumes we are silly children and we need to be supervised for our own good. The problem is that there is no greater power that can be asked to keep an eye on us, we are God—you can't go any higher. How would you feel if I said to you that you can't be trusted to drive a car safely and I am going to have someone else supervise all your future driving. Most people would be highly insulted and offended at the very suggestion. But only because mostly we all think we are very good drivers—it's the guy in the car in front of us who is a bloody idiot.

When you become experienced at tapping into the power of the universe and you reach the point where I am, when you believe with 100% conviction that the rockets you launch into the universe will hit their target, and while you may not know exactly how the intention will be delivered, but you do know with certainty that something beautiful is on the way, *then* you will feel the confidence and self-belief in your own freewill that you already feel about your ability to drive a car.

Q4. I asked the universe to let me find my soulmate but I keep ending up in bad relationships with the wrong people—what gives?

Here we have another question phrased from within the illusion of time. So you want to meet your soulmate? But, presumably you don't want to meet them and then completely mess it up and scare them away?

Of course not, so maybe you need to learn a few lessons first? Do not place timescales on your intentions; trust the universe to deliver your dreams when it is perfect for you and your soulmate and not a moment too early or too late. Maybe you are ready but your partner needs a few more lessons, or vice versa. If I had met Daniela five years ago, I would have still fallen instantly head over heels in love with her, but I know for a fact that I was not the man she needed me to be at that point. Our relationship would have been short, dramatic and very painful.

Just like your future relationship with your soulmate, your relationship with the universe should be built on a rock-solid foundation of trust and love.

Q5. If I worry about negative things, will I manifest them into my life?

You don't need to worry; your fleeting predictions of doom and gloom won't be manifested unless you go to great effort to apply your focus on them in a dedicated manner. If you spend four hours a day visualizing a terrible car crash then you are likely to be operating at a very low vibrational state and pulling negativity towards you, but it doesn't necessarily mean you will crash your car that week. If we only had to think of something and it would magically appear, we would have aircraft crashing all over the place, lions escaping from zoos every day and bosses dropping down dead every time they chastised an employee who was late for work.

Trust me on this, if you follow the guide I am about to explain to you, nothing but amazing events and people will be turning up in your life very soon.

The 421 Journal

Most people meander through life without bothering to write down their goals. Very few people have specific and measurable goals, and even fewer have written these goals down. An even smaller number have also thought of a specific plan to make these goals a reality.

But does writing down your goals really help, or is it just a myth? If it really helps, what's the best goal-setting strategy?

Forbes reports a remarkable study about goal-setting carried out in the Harvard MBA program. Harvard's graduate students were asked whether they had set clear, written goals for their futures, as well as whether they had made specific plans to transform their fantasies into realities.

The result of the study was that only 3% of the students had written goals and plans to accomplish them, 13% had goals in their minds but hadn't written them anywhere, and 84% had no goals at all.

After 10 years, the same group of students were interviewed again and the conclusion of the study was totally astonishing.

- The 13% of the class who had goals, but did not write them down, earned twice the amount of the 84% who had no goals.

- The 3% who had written goals were earning, on average, ten times as much as the other 97% of the class combined.

- People who don't write down their goals tend to fail more easily than people who have plans.

There is power in the pen, but it is not so much the fact that you have your wishes and desires written down but rather that you paused your busy life for a moment to focus 100% on thinking about what you want. Sure, you can daydream about what you want to manifest while you are making a cup of coffee, but how much of your focus is on the desire and how much is on not scalding yourself with the boiling water? When you sit down with a journal and a pen and think carefully about what you want in your life, it requires your sole concentration, or perhaps I should say your soul concentration.

You may have read other law of attraction books that water down the principle of this universal law into 'you get what you think about'. A lot of people try this and quickly become despondent when their dreams don't start showing up. Others manage some initial success but then lose momentum; the magic appears to wear off. This is all because the law of attraction is not so simple that you just have to think about what you want and it miraculously appears, and thank God it isn't. You would be having lions and tigers and bears turning up in your living room all the time if this were true, oh my!

The easiest way I can explain this to you is by asking you to imagine that we are all vessels or containers, similar to a water jug. If you start pouring water into the jug, there will quickly come a point at which the jug is full and no more water can be added. At this point you are left with two choices: you can leave the jug as it is, but in doing so allow the water to go stagnant, or you can pour some of the water out to make room for more to be added. It is the same with us, but instead of water, imagine the substance we contain is the power of the universe. If you constantly keep asking for more and more stuff to appear in your life, you will get to a point where your connection to source becomes stagnant. You will stop manifesting the life you desire because there simply isn't any more room in your vessel.

To live this beautiful life I am teaching about, you must be like a river and not like a dam. Love, money, success and happiness must be constantly flowing through your life. You can't expect to manifest your soulmate and then treat him or her badly. For you to find your perfect partner, the love you receive must be equal to the love you give. Otherwise the relationship will stagnate for one or both of you. This principle applies to everything you manifest using the law of attraction. If you hoard the extra money you create using the secrets of this book, eventually the universe will stop responding to your requests for more wealth. You will have become a blockage in the flow of money; source becomes aware that once money gets to you, it goes no further.

To ensure you get the balance right, I have spent a lot of time working on a way that you can always ensure you give back to source in sufficient quantity so that there is always water flowing into your vessel. Every morning I sit down with a cup of coffee and I open a very beautiful leather-bound notepad. Clipped to the side of this pad is a wonderfully elegant silver fountain pen. This daily diary is called my 421 Journal. If you are really serious about changing your life, I am suggest you do the same thing every day. Today go and buy a notepad and pen. I find it adds to the routine if you put a little care and attention into the writing materials you are going to be using. Buy a beautiful notebook and a pen that you like to write with. This routine is going to be an important and magical part of your day, so make sure it feels significant.

The number 421 refers to the balance of giving, sending and receiving you are going to be offering to the universe every day. It is important that you find a moment of peace and tranquility every day where you can do this. Your focus needs to be completely on the page. If the children are running around the kitchen while you are trying to write or your secretary keeps calling you at your desk, then your attention is broken. For example, this morning I got up at 5:30 am, long before my kids get up for school. I fed the dogs and cats and made myself a cup of coffee.

Then I sat in silence and opened my journal. I already knew what I was going to write because I had awoken a few times during the night with thoughts that I instantly decided needed to be in my diary for today.

At the top of a new page I wrote today's date, 29th April 2016. Next I started to write out four statements of things in my life that I am profoundly grateful for. I am away from my home in Cyprus at the moment, and I woke up to an SMS message from my partner Daniela that simply said "Good morning, I love you'. So the first line of my journal today states 'Thank you for the amazing loving relationship that Daniela and I enjoy so much'.

Next I write down two things in my awareness that need more love. I sent my love to my daughter, who is having a tough time at school at the moment, and also to a friend who today will have a biopsy on his lung to check for cancer.

Finally, I wrote down my intention for today, or if you prefer, my instruction to the universe of what I want delivered. This doesn't have to be an earth-shatteringly large request; it can be big or small. A steady stream of small manifestations is much more rewarding than taking risks with gigantic requests to win the lottery, etc. I have some good news and some bad news for you about this whole law of attraction thing. The bad news is that this is not Aladdin's lamp. You can't wish for anything and WHOOSH it magically appears. Imagine if ten thousand people bought this book and all on the same day they wrote 'I want to win the lottery today'. How can the universe generate that many winning tickets? And even if it did, the prize pool would be divided so many times that every single person would be left disappointed. You are asking the universe to push you in a direction rather than just hand stuff to you on a silver plate. If you ask to meet your soulmate, the universe will not create a new person from scratch (like in that movie *Weird Science*), but rather it will start moving two compatible people closer together, motivating you both to be at the same place at the same time and so on.

So you have had the bad news; now for the good. Unlike Aladdin's lamp you don't get just three wishes—you get 365 wishes. One a day for every day of the year. Before you ask… yes, you can ask for more than that, but I have found it is better to focus your intention on one a day. Otherwise you get lost in perpetually 'wanting'. When this happens, blockages start appearing. The 421 Journal is designed to put your primary focus on giving rather than on receiving. Each day's entry starts with four expressions of gratitude for what you already have in your life, two gifts of love for someone else and one cosmic order to the universe.

You will come to see this journal as something quite magical in your life, a sacred document. When I sit down to write in my own 421 Journal, I take the process very seriously. I make sure I am in a quiet place on my own, and before I put pen to paper I sit in silent contemplation for a few moments. I know that what I write in that book will become reality, so it is worth pausing just for a moment and focusing on what would serve me best.

There is no doubt in my mind that what I have asked for will be delivered, I know that the moment the intention is set, the outcome has already happened—even before the ink dries. All I have to do next is wait patiently for time to catch up. It's a bit like sending an ethereal email—once you click send you can't see where the message is on its journey, and you don't worry about which part of the Internet is currently hosting your communication. As soon as you click send an unbreakable chain of events begins. If you have ever sent an email to entirely the wrong (and most inappropriate) person, then you will know firsthand that it doesn't matter how many times you click cancel. That disastrous message has already delivered its payload.

Writing the *Manifesting Magic* series of books has been a big part of my life for over two years. It will be a little strange to open my laptop and not see an open document waiting for more of my cosmic ramblings. However, I am immensely grateful for the opportunity to share this wonderful knowledge with people around the world. I will close this book with a special 421 journal entry.

Sunday 1st May 2016

Gratitude

1. Thank you for the growing audience for this material and the opportunity to change lives around the world.

2. Thank you for the skills and experiences I have enjoyed over the years that have put me in the position to write like this.
3. Thank you for all the amazing emails and stories I get to hear from people around the world who have turned their lives around with this material.
4. I am so grateful that I continue to learn and grow as a person.

Love

1. I send love to the people reading this who really need something dramatic to change in their lives right now.
2. I send love to the people of the world who will never come in contact with this information and who live without even the basic necessities for life.

Order

1. Thank you for the great feedback, ratings and reviews that I see appearing all over the Internet for this book.

Until we meet and you tell me about all the amazing things that happened to you, I wish you all the happiness, peace and purpose that you desire.

Craig Beck

Recommended links:

- http://www.CraigBeck.com
- http://www.PowerfullyWealthy.com
- http://www.SubAttraction.com
- http://www.StopDrinkingExpert.com

Manifesting Magic Coaching Program

Do you want to be the next person to start living the life of their dreams?

www.craigbeck.com

Life is harsh right? But if you work long and hard you can ease the struggle... no pain, no gain!

Wrong, wrong, wrong! Virtually everything you have been told about how to have a happy, successful life is wrong. Not just a little bit wrong but the exact polar opposite of the truth!

So many people spend an entire lifetime not quite having enough... they get stuck in a job they don't like, in a relationship that isn't healthy and struggle along always with not quite enough money.

Life is not meant to be a struggle, money is not supposed to be scarce and you are not here to spend half your precious time on this planet working in a job that doesn't fulfill you and leaves you wondering what the point of it all is!

- *Yes I know you read 'The Secret' & it didn't work the way you hoped.*
- *Yes I know you tried positive thinking & found it impossible to maintain.*
- *Yes I know you have read self-help books & a hundred other things.*

Why didn't any of that work and why don't you have the life you dream of?

The truth has been sanitized to appeal to a mass market—remember, what I am about to show you flies in the face of what virtually everyone currently believes. Only a very select few people will be open-minded enough to be able to process this knowledge.

I do not advertise this website... Most people never find this coaching program; there is a reason you are here. You should trust me on this because a uniquely magical experience is just a mouse click away. Why not decide now and join my Manifesting Magic Coaching Program today?

I want you to be the next person whose life completely changes beyond their wildest dreams.

Part One

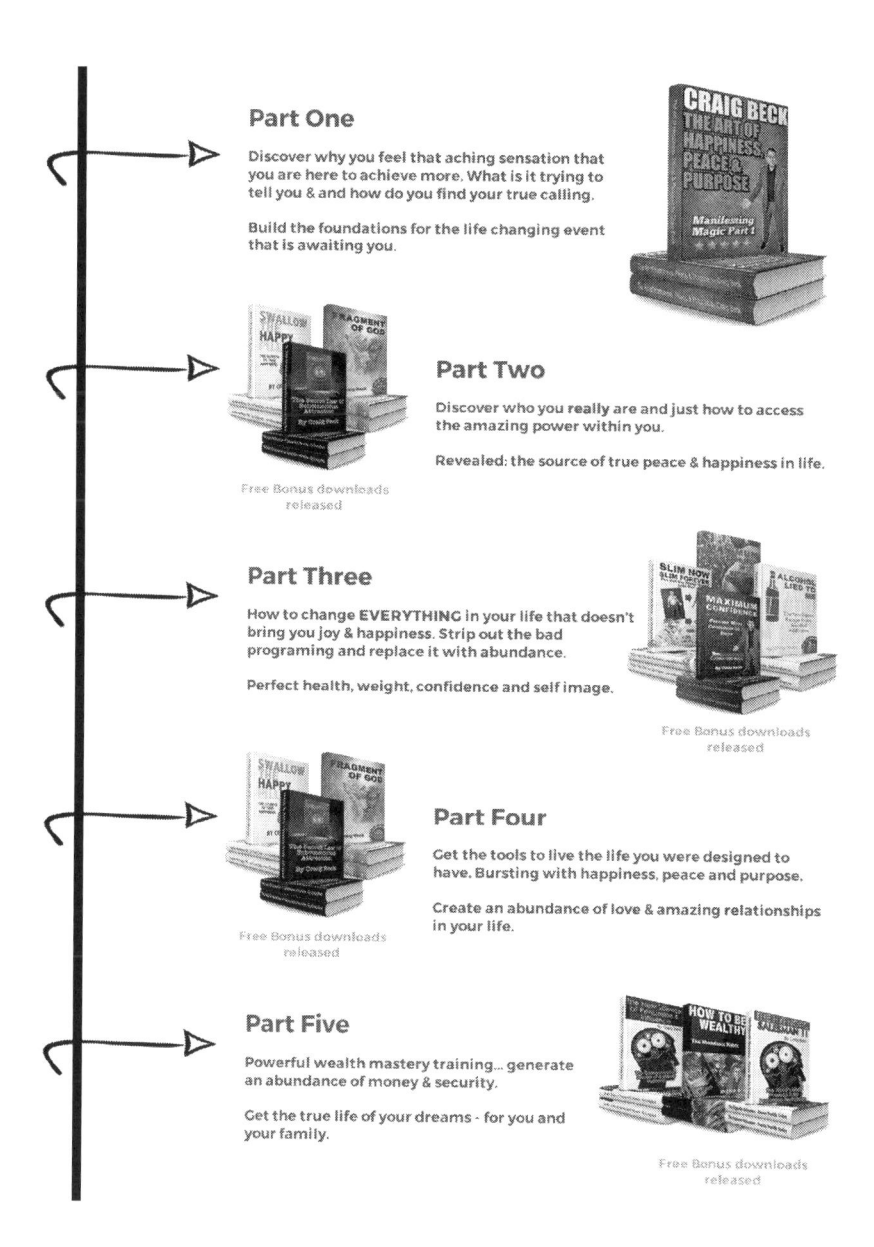

Discover why you feel that aching sensation that you are here to achieve more. What is it trying to tell you & and how do you find your true calling.

Build the foundations for the life changing event that is awaiting you.

Part Two

Discover who you **really** are and just how to access the amazing power within you.

Revealed: the source of true peace & happiness in life.

Free Bonus downloads released

Part Three

How to change **EVERYTHING** in your life that doesn't bring you joy & happiness. Strip out the bad programing and replace it with abundance.

Perfect health, weight, confidence and self image.

Free Bonus downloads released

Part Four

Get the tools to live the life you were designed to have. Bursting with happiness, peace and purpose.

Create an abundance of love & amazing relationships in your life.

Free Bonus downloads released

Part Five

Powerful wealth mastery training... generate an abundance of money & security.

Get the true life of your dreams - for you and your family.

Free Bonus downloads released

www.CraigBeck.com

Printed in Great Britain
by Amazon